PROFILES OF MODERN
AMERICAN AUTHORS

PROFILES OF MODERN
AMERICAN AUTHORS

by Bernard Dekle

★ ★ ★

CHARLES E. TUTTLE COMPANY
Rutland, Vermont   Tokyo, Japan

Representatives

Continental Europe: BOXERBOOKS, INC., *Zurich*
British Isles: PRENTICE-HALL INTERNATIONAL, INC., *London*
Australasia: PAUL FLESCH & CO., PTY. LTD., *Melbourne*
Canada: M. G. HURTIG, LTD., *Edmonton*

Published by the Charles E. Tuttle Company, Inc.
of Rutland, Vermont & Tokyo, Japan
with editorial offices at
Suido 1-chome, 2-6, Bunkyo-ku, Tokyo

Library of Congress Catalog Card No. 69-13504
Standard Book No. 8048 0491-5

First printing, 1969
Second printing, 1970

PRINTED IN JAPAN

TABLE OF CONTENTS

INTRODUCTION

THIS BOOK came about quite accidentally. While serving as Director of the American Cultural Center in Kobe, Japan, my staff and I often received requests for an easily understandable book on the lives of modern American authors. The basic facts, of course, about American writers were readily available: date and place of birth, education, marital status, most important works, and so on; all could easily be found in the encyclopedias. There were many critical studies, too, but practically all were scholarly works beyond the comprehension of Japanese still groping with the English language. Our biographical material on American authors, valuable

as it was, obviously did not fully meet the require-
ments of the young students. What they wanted was
a book of simply written, flesh-and-blood word
portraits. They wanted to know Walt Whitman,
Sinclair Lewis, Ernest Hemingway, Robert Frost,
and other American writers as living people: their
appearance, their dominant traits, their strengths
and weaknesses. Finding no such volume in our
library or in the book catalogues, I started writing
one. The result after more than ten years of research
and writing, principally on weekends when I could
spare time from my duties as a U.S. Government
Information Officer, is *Profiles of Modern American
Authors*.

The period covered by this book, roughly the
first half of the 20th century, is perhaps the most
significant in American literature. With the coming
of the new century, scientific advances had brought
rapid expansion of industry in the United States,
agrarian influence had declined, and the daily
life and thinking of millions of Americans were changing as old beliefs tagged to outworn philoso-
phies were discarded. Gone at last was the frontier
which from the days of the Pilgrims had exerted vast
influence on American letters. The time was ripe for
change. Authors who for generations had written

about America with one eye cocked on Europe had passed into history. The decline of isolationism and the growing awareness in Americans of their nation's strength and place in world affairs instilled new confidence in artists. Writers, especially, began to strike out in new directions. In every genre—fiction, poetry, and drama—authors no longer were content to follow familiar patterns. They introduced new and sometimes radical techniques which, although troublesome at first to readers accustomed to the old ways, gradually came to be accepted as fresh, vital, and important. For the first time America, like France and England, developed what could be called a distinct, well-rounded literature.

Innovators who contributed to the making of the new 20th-century American literature are predominant in this book. Most of the authors experimented with new forms or modes of expression which greatly influenced their contemporaries and later writers. Walt Whitman's free verse and sweeping cadences have been likened to a fresh breeze which swept the American continent. Stephen Crane, another trail blazer, scorned the fashionable, sentimental writing of his day and began chronicling the bare, unpleasant facts of life. Robert Frost, while adhering principally to established forms, scoffed at traditional poetical idealization of human existence, and chose to write mainly about the tragic aspects of life. Eugene O'Neill experimented widely, employing naturalistic, impressionistic, and stream-of-consciousness techniques. A dozen or more writers—Sherwood Anderson, Upton Sinclair, John P. Marquand, F. Scott Fitzgerald, Sinclair Lewis, John Dos Passos, John Steinbeck, and others—extended the frontiers of the realistic and naturalistic novel. Their voices, often critical, frequently screamed out against established institutions and ideologies, or protested against the economic and political system.

There has been no attempt to fit the authors whose profiles appear here into their respective niches in literature. Rather, it has seemed fit to present them as people, discuss their most significant works, and leave the assessment of their achievements to the critics—who, it will be noted, often have conflicting opinions about them. It can be said, however, to the credit of all of the 20th-century authors presented in this book, that not one accepted pat solutions as had many of their 19th-century predecessors; not one was guilty of narrow nationalism or chauvinism. All wrote not only for Americans, but for everyone, as if the entire world were listening.

Acknowledgment is gratefully made to the following

for permission to reprint selections included in this book:

The Atlantic Monthly for quotations from "Boy and Man from Sauk Centre" by Dorothy Thompson, November, 1960, and "John P. Marquand" by Edward A. Weeks, October, 1960;

Harcourt, Brace and World, Inc. for "it may not always be so" from *Poems 1923–1954* by E. E. Cummings, and an excerpt from *The Autobiography of Upton Sinclair;*

Harper and Row, Inc. for selections from *O'Neill* by Arthur and Barbara Gelb, and the "Good-by world" scene from Act 3 of *Our Town* by Thornton Wilder;

Holt, Rinehart and Winston, Inc. for "The Objection to Being Stepped On" and "Stopping by Woods on a Snowy Evening" from *The Complete Poems of Robert Frost;*

Irving Howe for quotations from "The Stature of Theodore Dreiser" and "Dreiser and the Tragedy" (*New Republic,* July 25 and August 22, 1964);

Alfred A. Knopf, Inc. for quotations from "My People," "The Weary Blues," and "Let America Be America Again" by Langston Hughes, and four excerpts from the poems of Wallace Stevens;

New Directions Publishing Corporation for quotations from "Spring Storm," "The Young Housewife," and "St. Francis of the Daffodils" from *The Collected*

Earlier Poems of William Carlos Williams, and "Cortege" from *In the Winter of Cities* by Tennessee Williams;

Saturday Review for two paragraphs from "From a Black Abyss, a Man and Artist" by Granville Hicks, April 7, 1962;

Charles Scribner's and Sons for quotations from *The Great Gatsby* by F. Scott Fitzgerald, *Look Homeward, Angel* by Thomas Wolfe, and *Dreiser* by W. A. Swanberg;

The Viking Press, Inc. for selections from the *Grapes of Wrath* by John Steinbeck and *Herzog* by Saul Bellow, and excerpts from an interview with William Faulkner in *Writers at Work,* edited by Malcolm Cowley.

BERNARD DEKLE

WALT WHITMAN

(1819–1892)

He Sang the Songs of the Commonplace

ALTHOUGH Walt Whitman wrote in the 19th century, his *Leaves of Grass,* the volume into which he put almost all his poetry, is far more 20th century in form and spirit than the work of the vast majority of American writers published today.

Whitman was born on May 31, 1819, in his grandfather's house, a small, wooden structure in a tiny community on Long Island, New York. His father was a day laborer and his mother could barely write her name. There were nine children, and none except Walt showed the slightest talent; but the family was so large, there was no chance to give him more than rudimentary education.

Walt Whitman's schooling ended at ten. At twelve he worked as a printer's apprentice. At thirteen he cleaned the press of a Long Island newspaper. At sixteen he supported himself on the few dollars he earned as a typesetter. Between seventeen and twenty the untaught youth managed to teach country schoolboys who knew even less than he did. At twenty he changed his occupation and decided to publish a newspaper. He bought a small, secondhand press and put out a paper in his home town, but he went broke after a year. He seemed unable to stick to any one job. For the next six years he worked on various newspapers until he was made editor of the *Brooklyn Eagle*.

Nothing written by Whitman during this period showed the slightest trace of genius. On the contrary, the editorials he wrote showed both immaturity and lack of talent. His poetry was almost unbelievably bad—commonplace, sentimental, stilted, and crammed with old-fashioned worn-out phrases.

Whitman left the *Brooklyn Eagle* after two years. At twenty-nine he again faced a bleak future. He had failed as a teacher, printer, journalist, and editor; but he refused to think of himself as a failure. He heard that a job was open on a newspaper in New Orleans and, with his fifteen-year-old brother, journeyed to Louisiana. He wrote articles about local subjects, but the owner of the New Orleans paper objected to Whitman's sympathy for the lower classes—rivermen, oyster vendors, stevedores, out-of-work laborers—and after a few months he was fired.

Back in Brooklyn and again unemployed, Whitman was now free to continue his experiments in writing which he had begun at intervals between his many jobs. He had jotted down over the years strange sentences, part poetry, part prose, altogether different from the clumsy verses he had written in the past. He was unable to sell his book to a publishing house, but in 1855 the owners of a small Brooklyn printshop allowed him to set up a volume of ninety-five pages, comprising twelve poems.

"Leaves of Grass"

He was proud of his little book, never imagining that there would be many editions and that its ninety-five pages would grow to more than four hundred. He wanted the book to be a democratic document, and he named it *Leaves of Grass* after the common grass which grows "wherever the land is."

The book received few reviews. Most were unpleasant. Several were abusive. A Boston paper found the book "an impertinence towards the English language." The *London Critic* concluded that the author was "as unaquainted with art as a hog is with mathematics."

The first note of approval came from the poet and sage Ralph Waldo Emerson. Without reservation, the famous Emerson wrote to the then-unknown poet as though he were writing to an established young artist. "I greet you," Emerson said in his letter, "at the beginning of a great career."

In *Leaves of Grass*, Whitman was exuberant. He glorified the things that are all about us; he made them wonderful, miracles of every day. He found marvels in what had always seemed commonplace.

> The commonplace I sing;
> How cheap is health! How cheap nobility!
> The open air I sing, freedom, toleration.

* * *

The common day and night—the common
  earth and waters,
Your farm—your work, trade, occupation,
The democratic wisdom underneath, like solid
  ground for all.

Male Nurse in Civil War

Meanwhile, Whitman's career had continued its irregular course—newspaper work alternating with manual labor and unemployment. But from the first publication of *Leaves of Grass*, he had a vocation. Instead of going on to write new books, he continued to work on the same one—adding new poems, revising old ones, and printing a new edition every few years. It was a process that was to continue all his life, with the final edition appearing in the year of his death.

In 1860 came the Civil War, and although Whitman did not enlist—considering himself too old—he became a male nurse, a comforter and caretaker of the wounded. No task was too menial or ugly for him. He washed the bodies of the afflicted; he carried bedpans; he dressed hideous wounds; and when the soldiers started to recover, he wrote letters for them, read to them, brought books, apples, and sugar to sweeten their stale coffee.

The new experiences gave him and his poetry more strength. It vibrated with comradely love. A new series of poems, *Drum Taps*, quivered with deeply moving intensity. His poem on the death of the martyred President, Abraham Lincoln, is considered one of the noblest elegies in the English language. It begins:

When lilacs last in the dooryard bloom'd,
And the great star early droop'd in the western
   sky in the night,
I mourn'd, and yet shall mourn with ever-
   returning spring.

*   *   *

Ever-returning spring, trinity sure to me you
   bring,
Lilac blooming perennial and drooping star
   in the west,
And thought of him I love.

Lonely and Ill

After the war, Whitman was employed for a time in government offices in Washington, D.C.; but in 1873, lonely and ill, he settled in Camden, New Jersey, where his mother and one of his brothers were living. Meanwhile, his reputation had spread not only throughout America but overseas. He was hailed by English critics and poets, notably Tennyson, Rossetti, Wilde, and Swinburne. Nevertheless, he was poor. The sale of his revised and expanded *Leaves of Grass* yielded little money, and he had to depend largely on an occasional dollar from peddling his books and contributions from his friends. Once the American philanthropist Andrew Carnegie sent him a check for $350, saying: "Whitman is the greatest poet of democracy so far."

In his sixty-ninth year, Whitman suffered a renewal of the illness which had afflicted him after the war. He rallied for a time and, although feeble, was able to attend a celebration in honor of his seventieth birthday, but after that he did not appear in public. He died of pneumonia on March 26, 1892, at the age of seventy-two.

Glory of the Commonplace

Seldom has the glory of the commonplace been so symbolized in a single poem as in the lines which Whitman called "Miracles." The poem in part reads:

> Why, who makes much of a miracle?
> As to me, I know of nothing else but miracles. . . .
> To me every hour of the light and dark is a miracle,
>
> Every cubic inch of space is a miracle. . . .
> To me the sea is a continual miracle,
> The fishes that swim—the rocks—the motion of
> the waves—the ships with men in them—
> What stranger miracles are there?

The concept of Whitman's major work, *Leaves of Grass*, may be summed up in his simple and direct appeal to the reader:

> Camerado! This is no book.
> Who touches this touches a man.

This was Whitman's way of saying that all that he was, all that he had become from his lowly beginning, he had put into *Leaves of Grass*.

—Bibliography—

PRINCIPAL WORKS: *Leaves of Grass*, 1855; Complete Prose Works (all the poet said he wished to be preserved), 1892; *The Complete Writings of Walt Whitman*, 1902.

STEPHEN CRANE (1871–1900)

The Red Badge of Courage

In a brilliant and rebellious career that ended tragically at the age of twenty-nine, Stephen Crane left behind a legacy rarely equaled by a young author cut off at the height of his powers. Crane not only wrote *The Red Badge of Courage*, which is often called the best novel written about the Civil War, but—perhaps even more significant—his realistic approach to life, which scorned the fashionable sentimental writing of his day, marked the beginning of modern American fiction.

Crane's passion for reflecting the unpleasant facts of life, displayed in *The Red Badge* and other works, makes him the literary ancestor of such widely known later authors as John Dos Passos and Ernest Hemingway. In another field, his bluntly intense poems made him a pathfinder for poets devoted to experimental reform and revolt from sentimentality.

19

In Full Revolt

Born in New Jersey in 1871, the fourteenth child of a Methodist minister and an ardently religious mother, Crane grew up in full revolt against the restraints of conformity and his home environment. After studying briefly at Lafayette College in Pennsylvania and Syracuse University in New York, Crane plunged into a hand-to-mouth existence as a freelance reporter in New York City. For five hard and hungry years he was an apprentice writer, sharpening his skills and observing with a clear reporter's eye the life of social outcasts in a great city.

Crane's writing genius transformed the raw material of observation into his first novel, *Maggie: A Girl of the Streets*, the story of a girl driven to prostitution and suicide by poverty and sweatshop labor. The novel was so harsh a picture of a degenerate slum family that it shocked the genteel society of the day, and Crane was forced to publish it privately under another name. A financial failure and marred by immature writing, *Maggie* nevertheless pioneered America's entrance into naturalistic fiction and launched Crane on a career as a serious writer.

The rebellion against conformity that began in Crane's childhood and led him to the slums of New York lasted all of his life. He never married, but his varied and unconventional love affairs included a woman already engaged to another man, a married woman who later obtained a divorce, an actress, and the twice-married hostess of a nightclub who lived with him during the last three years of his brief life.

Famous at Twenty-four

He became famous at twenty-four with the publication of *The Red Badge of Courage*. Stressing the irony of chance that can make a man weak in the midst of impersonal and overwhelming forces, Crane limited his point of view to that of a common soldier, dramatizing the soldier's bewilderment as he overcame his initial cowardice. The story involves not only the conflict between Confederate and Union soldiers, but also the conflict in the mind of the soldier.

The Red Badge evokes the clamor and terror of death on the battlefield, creating an impressionistic picture of ordinary soldiers that perhaps no factual account could give. As a psychological study of the mind of a man under extreme tension and anxiety, the novel has few superiors. Crane's contemporary, author and critic Ambrose Bierce, noted for his sharp judgments of other writers, spoke highly of him. "This young man," Bierce wrote, "has the power to feel. He knows nothing of war but he is drenched in blood. Most beginners who deal with this subject matter spatter themselves with ink." Even professional military men were struck by the book's authentic tone. Such knowledge, they felt, could have come only from experience.

Revolutionary both in style and in its attitude toward war, *The Red Badge* cut through the flag-waving and the stirring music to expose war's filth, blood, and stench. The novel's matter-of-fact style was a mask for rage at social injustice, for Crane took bitter interest in deflating the myth that war is all glory and bravery.

Attracted by Violence and Death

Although he had not seen war when *The Red Badge* was written, Crane was later attracted again and again by violence and death. In 1895 he joined an expedition to invade Spanish-held Cuba, as a war correspondent. He never reached Cuba, for his ship was wrecked off the coast of Florida. Out of this experience came his most famous short piece, "The Open Boat," hailed by British writer H. G. Wells as "the finest short story in the English language."

Two years later, Crane had his first opportunity to compare his mental picture of war with the real thing. In 1897, Greece and Turkey went to war, and he was assigned as a war correspondent. He attached himself to the Greek Army and traveled with it, writing dispatches about battles, evacuations, hospitals, soldiers, civilians, deserted villages, stray dogs—whatever met his eyes. Finding that his experience of actual warfare confirmed what he had already seen in his acute visual imagination, he asserted, "*The Red Badge* was all right."

When the Spanish-American War began a year later, Crane returned to the United States to volunteer for service in the Navy. He was turned down, but again he became a war correspondent and covered campaigns in Cuba and in Puerto Rico.

One great virtue shines through his war dispatches: he was not pretending to be a recording device, an expert, or a chronicler who kept his emotions apart from his words. He wrote frankly his reaction and opinions about the debris of war—he mused over the body of a young soldier, ached for old refugees, criticized high commands, talked to soldiers. In his dispatches, there is the freshness of a lone intelligence—cool and ironic, yet capable of great anger and compassion—making cold news into human events.

Crane's dedicated pursuit of experience took its toll. His expenses far exceeded his income from writing, and, besieged by creditors, he tried desperately to write himself out of debt. But privations and illnesses suffered during his campaigns had already undermined his health. Suffering from tuberculosis, he collapsed early in April, 1900. At the advice of doctors, he left for Badenweiler, Germany, where he died a few weeks later.

Significance in American Literature

Many have believed Crane's early death was caused by the neglect of his contemporaries, but biographer R. W. Stallman has pointed out that no man of Crane's generation was more admired or received greater critical recognition. What killed him was not literary neglect, but his own will to burn himself out—to make his body a testing ground for all of life's sensations. Crane felt that the nearer a writer gets to life, the greater he becomes as an artist. Just like his pioneering work in naturalism, Crane's conviction that a concentrated search for experience must be part of the artist's creed had a decided impact on later American writers. This belief has influenced the life and work of many novelists writing today.

Crane's best stories concentrate on single acts of heroism and cowardice, and on the confused senses of bewildered individuals in crisis. His is a world of victims, and his work usually presents a man standing terrified before the inevitability of pointless death or inescapable humiliation. Every major story is designed upon a single ironic incident and all end with irony. His novels, short stories, and poetry all reflect the same naturalistic pessimism.

Like his friend, the great English writer Joseph Conrad, Crane realized that men doomed to destruction will often commit acts of bravery and sacrifice despite harsh consequences—that they may warm their hands for a moment at each other's humanity before whirling off to destruction.

—Bibliography—

PRINCIPAL WORKS: *Maggie: A Girl of the Streets*, 1893; *The Red Badge of Courage*, 1895; *The Black Riders* (poems), 1895; *The Monster and Other Stories*, 1899; *Wounds in the Rain*, 1900.

JACK LONDON

The Call of the Wild

ONE DAY in 1893, a seventeen-year-old American youth stood at the wheel of the sailing vessel *Sophie Sutherland,* an 80-ton schooner bound for the coast of Japan on a seal-hunting expedition. Three days out of San Francisco, the vessel ran into a typhoon. Her great sails were reefed as mountainous seas began to strike her broadside. Soon she began to wallow in the deep trough of the waves as though she was rocked in a gigantic cradle.

A few months later the young sailor, Jack London, who was to become one of America's most popular writers in the early 20th century, described the storm in these words:

"The sea was a dark lead color, as with long, slow, majestic roll it was heaped by the wind into a liquid mountain of foam. The wild antics of the schooner were sickening as she forged along. She would almost stop, as though climbing a mountain, then rapidly rolling to right and left as she gained the summit of a huge sea. Like an avalanche she shot forward and down as the sea astern struck her with the force of a thousand battering rams."

Wins Newspaper Contest

This graphic description of the typhoon-tossed schooner was part of an essay which the seventeen-year-old youth submitted in a newspaper contest. He won first prize, a remarkable achievement for young Jack London, especially since he had little schooling. More important still, the essay gave the world its first glimpse of the talent which within a few years was to make the young adventurer a famous author.

Jack London was born on January 12, 1876, in San Francisco, California, the illegitimate son of Flora Wellman and William Chaney, an itinerant writer, teacher, and astrologer. The couple separated soon after he was born, and within a few months Flora married a widower named John London. Flora's baby boy, Jack, took his stepfather's name of London.

A series of misfortunes brought the London family to a state of grinding poverty in the slums of Oakland, a suburb of San Francisco. Early in life the boy became the principal wage earner. Later, in a short biographical letter to his editor, Jack wrote:

"From my ninth year, with the exception of the years spent in school, my life was one of toil. It is worthless to give the long, sordid list of occupations, none of them trades, all heavy manual labor."

One Great Happiness

He did have one great happiness as a youth—the Oakland Public Library.

"I read everything, but principally history and adventure, and all the old travels and voyages. I read mornings, afternoons, and nights. I read in bed. I read at the table. I read as I walked to and from school, and I read at recess while the other boys were playing."

But there was always the desperate need for money, so Jack went from one back-breaking job to another—iceman's helper, cannery worker, coal heaver, longshoreman—all part of that long sordid list, as he called it. At fourteen he left school—and at fifteen decided to make his living on the water. The nearest body of water was San Francisco Bay.

"I was a salmon fisher, an oyster pirate, a schooner sailor, a fish patrolman, and a general sort of bay-faring adventurer—a boy in years and a man amongst men."

London Proves His Manhood

It was during the seal-hunting voyage on the *Sophie Sutherland* that Jack proved his manhood. But the urge for adventure still egged him on. He joined a crowd of unemployed men on a protest march to Washington, D.C.; he tramped about the country, begging food, sleeping in parks; he was finally imprisoned for vagrancy near Niagara Falls, New York. Back home, his mind made up to become a writer, he decided that he needed more schooling. So he studied furiously for a few weeks, easily passed the University of California entrance examinations—but spent only one semester in college.

"I found it impossible," he said. "Life and pocketbook were both too short."

But the greatest adventure of Jack London's early youth was still to come—his expedition to Alaska and the Klondike. The time was the Yukon River gold strike of 1897, and he was dazzled by the stories of fortunes being made. He dreamed of buying himself a literary career with Klondike gold.

Jack London found no gold, but he gained a greater fortune than gold during his year in Alaska—he accumulated a rich supply of ideas on which his future was to be based. He started to write as soon as he returned home, but a year of discouragement followed. Suddenly his luck changed. First, a magazine of great prestige accepted his story "An Odyssey of the North." Soon afterward a leading publisher offered him a contract for his book of short stories, *The Son of the Wolf: Tales of the Far North.*

"He draws vivid pictures of the terrors of cold, darkness, and starvation, the pleasures of human companionship in adverse circumstances. . . . The reader is convinced that the author has lived the life himself," one editor commented.

Early Success

Successful in his early twenties, Jack began to receive attention in literary and social circles. Proud rather than ashamed of his background of poverty, he was a stimulating companion. Richard O'Conner, a recent biographer, says:

"To watch Jack stride into a room, usually in a black turtleneck sweater, his hair tousled, his blue eyes glittering with mischief or excitement, was like having a window thrown open on a room thick with tobacco smoke. . . ."

In 1900, Jack London published his first novel—and he married Bess Maddern. In the next three years he wrote six more books, made more money than he ever dreamed of having, and was able to provide a fine home for his own family, and for his mother. He was not a happy man, however—he felt a strong sense of guilt because he was so successful while so many people in the world were poor. He visited England, spent six weeks living in the slums of the great city of London, and produced a book he called *The People of the Abyss*, more a sociological study than a novel.

Short Story Becomes a Novel

Home again, quieter and more confident—and cutting down on his drinking, which had been heavy since his teens —London began work on his great sea tragedy, *The Sea-Wolf*. He also started what he intended to be a short story, about a civilized dog suddenly thrust into the arctic wilderness and made to fight for survival. This story ran away from its author and became a novel, *The Call of the Wild*. Richard O'Conner's biography notes:

"Some reviewers paid him the ultimate compliment of the time by saying *The Call of the Wild* was as good as anything Kipling ever wrote. . . . Jack had finally struck the chord that awakened the fullest response in American readers. The book was translated into numerous languages and made its author world-famous."

But in that year of his greatest literary success, Jack London's private life became a public scandal. He left his wife and daughters for another woman, Charmian Kittridge. After his divorce he married Charmian, but the second marriage did not hold the happiness he had expected. Charmian was less loving and understanding than he had anticipated—she in turn found him difficult and demanding. His drinking became excessive, and she could see tragic consequences.

Fled to the Country

In his constant search for contentment, Jack retreated to the country, buying a great ranch, which he called the Valley of the Moon. He built a magnificent house which burned down before he ever lived in it. He built a boat in which he and Charmian cruised the South Seas. He traveled widely and for a change of pace he took an assignment to cover the Mexican Revolution as a news correspondent. He continued to write prolifically, short stories and novels that kept the money rolling in—money badly needed to pay for his own expensive way of life and to support his mother, his first wife, and his two daughters.

By 1916, with fifty books behind him—the last three not very successful—he became convinced that he was losing his grip on the public taste. One contemporary wrote:

"Success went sour, money slipped away from him, even recognition was emphemeral—and romantic love was the greatest fallacy of all."

Commits Suicide

On the night of November 21, 1916, Jack London brought his own life to an end with an overdose of the opiate his doctor had prescribed to relieve the pain of illness. He was only forty when he died.

His own life story, his consciously created legend, was an even greater legend than any he committed to paper.

—Bibliography—

PRINCIPAL WORKS: *The Son of the Wolf: Tales of the Far North*, 1900; *The People of the Abyss*, 1903; *The Call of the Wild*, 1903; *The Sea-Wolf*, 1904; *The Cruise of the Snark, 1911; The Valley of the Moon*, 1913.

ROBERT FROST (1874–1963)

Poetry Came Naturally

On an unpaved country road near the Middlebury River in the state of Vermont is a simple, slab farmhouse. There until his death in 1963 at the age of almost ninety lived Robert Frost, whom many regard as America's greatest 20th-century poet.

Robert Frost looked like a farmer and was a farmer. In his later years his rugged appearance, unruly white hair, dress and manner seemed to blend with the outdoor life. On his rocky, stiff New England soil he grew corn, peas, and potatoes.

Poetry came naturally to Robert Frost, like breathing and sleeping. Commenting on his writing, he once said: "I've always been writing. Not in a professional way— never had a desk, never had a room. Nearly everything I wrote in one sitting."

Some might think that in this busy machine age, poets would be neglected. But on Robert Frost's eighty-eighth birthday, the late President John F. Kennedy invited him to the White House in Washington. "We are proud of you; you represent the best in the United States," President Kennedy told Frost, presenting him with a congressional gold medal in recognition of his poetry—which, Kennedy said, "has enriched the culture of the United States and the philosophy of the world."

Frost was no stranger to Washington. When President Kennedy was inaugurated on January 20, 1961, the New England poet took part in the ceremony, reciting one of his poems, "The Gift Outright," a poem in which Frost sees true love of country as "salvation in surrender" to the land. On another occasion, he was invited to read some of his poems at the White House.

Robert Frost was born in San Francisco on March 26, 1874. His father, a renegade from a conservative New England family, was a pleasure-loving, free-spending journalist and politician. His mother was Scottish, a teacher and a devout Christian, and was fond of reading and reciting poetry to young Frost and his sister, Jeanie. When Frost was eleven, his father, who drank heavily, died of tuberculosis and his mother returned with her two children to New England where, with the help of her husband's family, she started a school.

School Poet

Robert Frost showed early literary talent. He wrote his first poetry in high school, later becoming editor of the school paper, senior-class poet, and valedictorian of his graduating class. Recognizing his talent, his grandparents sent him to Dartmouth College, but he rebelled against the discipline of college life. After this came a period of wandering, with Frost making a living teaching elementary school and doing odd jobs. Meanwhile, he continued to write poetry and while working as a mill hand wrote his first significant poem, "My Butterfly," which drew its inspiration, as its title suggests, from nature and is written in Frost's distinctive, down-to-earth idiom.

A year after "My Butterfly" was published, Frost married his high school sweetheart, Elinor White. She encouraged him to continue his education and he entered Harvard University, again sent by his grandparents. But college life was not for Frost; he was too restless. In his sophomore year he became seriously ill and was sent home to die, but recovered. Abandoning any further attempt to acquire a formal college education, he moved with his wife to a small farm at Derry, Massachusetts, given them by his grandparents.

Little to Eat

The Frosts could barely sustain themselves on their farm. Often they had only potatoes to eat. Luckily, however, villagers nearby heard a minister read one of Frost's poems and gave him a job in the village school.

Although Frost had begun writing poetry at the age of fifteen, fame and success came to him late. From 1912 to 1915 he lived in England—the only lengthy period he ever spent outside his beloved New England—and it was there, when he was almost forty, that his first two books were published. *A Boy's Will*, a collection of poems written in his teens, and *North of Boston*, poetic anecdotes and tales about New England life, established him as a great new American poet. Returning to the U. S., he found himself famous.

Frost's poetic material in these volumes and most of his other work was often taken directly from the hard and lonely life of the New England farmer, whom he knew well and whose psychology and turns of speech he accurately recorded in his verse. Frost's poetry reveals experience of universal implication and feelings of great depth. From his farm in Vermont came this poem "The Objection to Being Stepped On" from his last book, *In the Clearing*, released on his eighty-eighth birthday:

> At the end of the row
> I stepped on the toe
> Of an unemployed hoe.
> It rose in offence
> And struck me a blow
> In the seat of my sense.
> It wasn't to blame
> But I called it a name.
> And I must say it dealt
> Me a blow that I felt
> Like malice prepense.
> You may call me a fool,
> But was there a rule
> The weapon should be
> Turned into a tool?
> And what do we see?
> The first tool I step on
> Turned into a weapon.

It is a simple poem of a farmer stepping on a hoe that flies up and hits him on the head. But the meaning is deep; if innocent people are stepped on, they hit back, just as does the idle hoe whose toe gets stepped on.

Also typical of Robert Frost's simple, homespun poetry, but in a more serious vein, is "Stopping by Woods on a Snowy Evening" from his collection of verse *New Hampshire:*

> Whose woods these are I think I know.
> His house is in the village though;
> He will not see me stopping here
> To watch his woods fill up with snow.
>
> My little horse must think it queer
> To stop without a farmhouse near
> Between the woods and frozen lake
> The darkest evening of the year.
>
> He gives his harness bells a shake
> To ask if there is some mistake.
> The only other sound's the sweep
> Of easy wind and downy flake.
>
> The woods are lovely, dark and deep.
> But I have promises to keep,
> And miles to go before I sleep,
> And miles to go before I sleep.

Frost's great appeal to his fellow Americans, which in his latter years amounted to veneration, perhaps lay in his projection of a kind of father image—the image of what Americans think a poet should look like and be: homespun, self-reliant, Yankee-shrewd and full of mellow, ripe wisdom which only the hoary, patriarchial old age Robert Frost achieved could bring.

—Bibliography—

PRINCIPAL WORKS: *A Boy's Will*, 1913; *North of Boston*, 1914; *A Mountain Interval*, 1916; *New Hampshire*, 1923; *West-running Brook*, 1928; *A Further Range*, 1936; *A Witness Tree*, 1942; *A Masque of Reason*, 1945; *A Masque of Mercy*, 1947; *Steeple Bush*, 1947, *Complete Poems*, 1949; *In the Clearing*, 1961.

THEODORE DREISER   (1871–1945)

A Tortured Life

THEODORE DREISER is probably the most puzzling figure in
20th-century American literature. No other author of his
stature has survived so much hostile criticism or displayed
so much paradoxical thinking. Yet despite his inconsist-
encies and blunders, Dreiser's place in modern American
literature seems firmly established. His influence on the
naturalistic American novel has been enormous; moreover,
there is in his writings a peculiar power and honesty seldom
found elsewhere.

"No common man am I!" crowed Dreiser. Indeed he
was not. He stood 1.98 meters (6 feet, 6 inches) and looked
like a gangling Gargantua: lowering brows, a cast in one
eye, rubbery sprawling lips, and a slide-away chin. He was
often called a braggart, a plagiarist, a liar, and a bully. He
threw coffee in publisher Horace Liveright's face and once

challenged Sinclair Lewis to a duel. All his life Dreiser was an incorrigible, considered by many to be untrustworthy on almost every conceivable count.

His Life

Theodore Dreiser was born in Terre Haute, Indiana on August 27, 1871. The son of a desperately poor and narrowly religious family, Dreiser developed intense feelings about poverty and social restraint which showed clearly in all of his works. Dreiser's father was a religious fanatic who rarely worked, while his mother was quite the opposite— a warm-blooded, carefree woman who rarely worried. There were ten children in the Dreiser family, most of them undisciplined and on the wild side. One of them, Paul, was destined for fame as a song writer under the name of Paul Dresser. Lonely, nervous Theodore clung to his mother's skirts and suckled on fantasies of success. Restless to realize his ambition, he dropped out of high school after one year, worked sporadically, somehow managed to get into Indiana State University and then dropped out after only one year there.

"I seethed to express myself," he said, "deciding that newspaper work offered my best chance of success—the chance to rub shoulders with bankers, millionaires, artists, and executive leaders, the real rulers of the world." He worked as a reporter on the *Chicago Daily Globe* in 1892, then moved on to a succession of papers in St. Louis, Pittsburg, and New York City. During the next few years, Dreiser supported himself as an editor of various New York magazines. Meanwhile he was sharpening his skills by writing in his spare time.

"Sister Carrie"

His first novel, *Sister Carrie* (1900), produced such a storm of protest from readers and critics that his publisher withdrew it. *Carrie* tells the story of a beautiful but mercenary girl who, rather than work, chooses to live on the earnings of her lover. The novel exhibits most of Dreiser's merits and faults: the clumsy writing, the overpowering earnestness, the loose construction, and the massing of realistic detail. The critics cut it to ribbons: "immoral," "dreary," "a philosophy of despair." When the book sold only 456 copies and was withdrawn, Dreiser collapsed into paranoic delusions and contemplated suicide.

In 1907, however, *Carrie* was republished and acclaimed "a work of genius." Dreiser found himself in great demand. He took over as top editor of a nationally famous fashion magazine only to lose his job when he tried to seduce the daughter of an assistant editor. In the next five years he toured Europe, fought with his publisher, lived off advances —and agonizingly, determinedly labored to produce other novels: *Jennie Gerhardt, The Financier, The Titan,* and his autobiographical *The "Genius."* By 1916 Dreiser was the hero of the avant-garde and the pet peeve of the conservatives, who denounced *The "Genius"* as literary trash and got it banned by the censor. Crushed, Dreiser fell silent for ten years.

"An American Tragedy"

Better fortune, however, lay ahead. In 1925 *An American Tragedy* was published, establishing Dreiser as a literary hero. The story of a naïve young man in a hurry who murders his pregnant mistress so he can marry the boss's daughter, the book was acclaimed by critic Joseph Wood Krutch as "the greatest American novel of our generation." Within a year it made Dreiser $40,000 in royalties and $80,000 in film rights.

The controlling pattern in *An American Tragedy* and other Dreiser novels has been well described by Bernard Rosenberg, a sociologist with a literary eye:

"Emile Durkheim, the social critic, had suggested in Dreiser's day that when men speak of a force external to themselves which they are powerless to control, their subject is not God but social organization. This is also Dreiser's theme, and to it he brings a sense of religious awe and wonder. 'So well defined,' he writes, 'is the sphere of social activity that he who departs from it is doomed.' . . . Durkheim identified social facts, for example, the existence of norms, precisely as Dreiser did: by asking what would happen if they were violated. . . . Norms develop outside the individual consciousness and exist prior to it; we internalize them and are fully aware of their grip only when our behavior is deviant. Durkheim illustrated this proposition in a dozen different ways, and so did Dreiser."

Theodore Dreiser was neither a clear nor an original thinker. Though he assimilated many of the ideas of the evolutionists, he remained enough of a skeptic to show marked ambiguities in his work. He is both a determinist and a sentimentalist; evoking considerable pity for his defeated characters. He appears to believe that it is proper for a man to grab as much as possible from an indifferent or malevolent society. The main theme in Dreiser's work is that of the conflict between the individual and society. In keeping with this theme, his characters are typically either weaklings or else strong figures who seize what they want.

Dreiser's Awards

In 1941 the League of American Writers gave Dreiser the first award of the Randolph Bourne Medal as the American writer who had performed the most distinctive service for culture and peace. The American Academy of Arts and Letters awarded him its Merit Medal for Fiction in 1944.

Dreiser died of a heart attack in Hollywood, California on December 28, 1945. Biographer W. A. Swanberg said this of Dreiser:

"... The liar who demanded truth in the world; the hater who called for love; the money-grubber who denounced capital; the glorifier of the proletariat who held the mass in contempt; the ego so vast that it exempted only himself from his own standards; the boy who never really reached maturity and yet who exuded at times a charm and sympathy that is warmly remembered to this day."

Friend of Mencken

At the time of Dreiser's death, H. L. Mencken, one of Dreiser's earliest and most devoted friends, and one of the first to be alienated, wrote:

"While Dreiser lived, all the literary popinjays of the country devoted themselves to reminding him of his defects. He had, to be sure, a number of them. For one thing, he came into the world with an incurable antipathy for the *mot juste;* for another thing, he had an insatiable appetite for the obviously not true. But the fact remains that he was a great artist, and that no other American of his generation left so wide and handsome mark upon national letters."

Whether Dreiser was actually a great artist has been much debated, but his historical importance is undeniable. He looked on life as none of his predecessors had done, and he was not afraid to tell what he saw. Dreiser led a tortured life, but he made something out of his torments.

Although it now seems certain that his reputation will endure, it is difficult to forecast what final judgment the critics and literary historians will pass on him. It is hard to measure a giant.

—Bibliography—

PRINCIPAL WORKS: *Sister Carrie*, 1900; *Jennie Gerhardt*, 1911; *The Financier*, 1912; *The Titan*, 1914; *The "Genius,"* 1915; *An American Tragedy*, 1925; *The Stoic*, 1947.

SINCLAIR LEWIS (1885–1951)

Novelist of Satire

In 1913, a gangling, red-haired young reporter was fired
by both the Associated Press and the San Francisco *Bulletin*
for incompetency. Seven years later, at the age of thirty-
five, the same man wrote a best-selling novel. A decade
after the publication of that novel, the man, Sinclair Lewis,
became the first American to win the Nobel prize for literature, the world's most coveted literary award which brings
immediate fame and fortune to its receiver.

It is ironic that Lewis, who lost his job as a reporter because of incompetency, should later achieve fame through
the realism of his novels. For undoubtedly his reportorial
skill—his ability to write with great accuracy and sharp
detail about the people, places, and events of his day—
contributed much to Sinclair Lewis' remarkable success
as a novelist.

44

Born in Small Town

Sinclair Lewis was born on February 7, 1885, in the small town of Sauk Centre, Minnesota. The third son of a country doctor, he grew to be a thin-faced, big-nosed, deeply freckled youth—unattractive features which helped to make his boyhood a lonely one. To help relieve this loneliness, which was to plague him throughout his life, he kept a diary in which he wrote about the sights and events in his home town. This diary was undoubtedly a source for much of his early writing.

From high school, "Red" Lewis went on to Yale University. Even there he was, at least in his own mind, an outcast. So once again he took to writing. But this time, instead of keeping a diary, he wrote for and later became editor of the Yale literary magazine. After graduating in 1908, Lewis drifted to New York and tried to earn a living by free-lance writing, but without success. He then began almost two years of wandering, mostly in the East and West, working as a reporter for a newspaper in Iowa and for a charity organization in New York. Finally he sold a story to a magazine, using the proceeds to go to California. It was while there that he was fired by the Associated Press and one of the city's big daily newspapers, the *Bulletin*.

Still determined to become a writer, Lewis again tried his luck in New York and things began to look up. He got a job with a publishing house, advancing from a manuscript writer to assistant editor and then to editor. He worked as editor, meanwhile continuing to write fiction, until 1916, when as the author of two published novels and a half dozen stories, he decided to try his hand once more at free-lance writing. It was not, however, until four years

later when *Main Street* was published in 1920 that real success came. The book quickly became a best seller, bringing
with it wide acclaim for its author.

Spokesman for Realism

The next ten years saw Lewis at his best, and most of his
important novels were written during that period. He became a literary hero and America's chief spokesman for
realism in literature. The decade was climaxed by the pres-
entation to Lewis of the Nobel prize for literature in December of 1930, marking the first time an American had won
that coveted award.

Soon afterward, however, interest in Lewis' novels began
to decline, and the period from the late 1930's until his
death in 1951 was one of decreasing popularity. During
most of that period he lived in Europe. In 1942 his marriage
to Dorothy Thompson, the well-known American journalist, ended in divorce. With the completion of his last novel,
World So Wide, in Florence, Italy, in early 1950, Lewis set
out on what was intended to be a long trip throughout
Europe; but after three months of travel, illness forced him
to settle in Rome, where he worked at writing poetry until
he died.

"Main Street"

Until Lewis' success with *Main Street* in 1920, he was just
another run-of-the-mill storyteller, his novels and stories
conforming to current popular standards of his time. It was
only when he decided to break loose and write a novel for
his own pleasure—saying just what he thought, whether it
pleased other people or not—that *Main Street* was produced.

Along with the wide popularity of *Main Street* came a storm of controversy, which worried Lewis not at all. The controversy was directed at his portrait of life and people in Gopher Prairie, a fictitious, small, and supposedly typical midwestern town in Minnesota.

Using the knowledge gained in his youth, spent in a town similar to the one in his novel, Lewis shattered forever the sentimental tradition clinging to American village life. He attempted to puncture the egos of people who consider their home towns flawless, and also to present an accurate picture of an important part of American society of his day.

He did this by tracing the life of the story's heroine, Carol Kennicott, an idealist intent upon reforming not only her husband, a doctor in Gopher Prairie, but also the town itself. After living there for several years and finding most of her attempts unsuccessful, Carol leaves the town and her husband and takes up residence in a large city, only to discover that the people there are but an accumulation of the population of thousands of Gopher Prairies all over the nation. She finally returns home and for the first time begins to feel serene, realizing at last that Gopher Prairie is where she belongs and where she wants to be.

Voice of Protest

Lewis used the background of his own home town in writing *Main Street*, but for his later novels he worked hard to familiarize himself with the settings where his stories were to take place. For one novel he studied the business of real estate; for another the life of a minister. He drew up detailed biographies of all the principal characters that filled his books and compiled statistics on the towns they lived in. He had a sharp eye for characteristic detail and an ear for actual American speech which, added to his careful preparation, gave to his novels a solid reality.

Because of this gift for bringing segments of America vividly to life, Lewis became one of the strongest voices of protest against certain of these segments. He took aim at many aspects of society in the 1920's and his satires dealing with the business world *(Babbitt)*, professional medicine *(Arrowsmith)*, and organized religion *(Elmer Gantry)*, brought him his greatest success.

"Babbitt"

A good example of his type of protest is the novel *Babbitt*, considered by many to be his best work. It is a clear and brilliant photograph of small-city business society. In it, Lewis describes how individuality is lost through group conformity. Since publication of the novel, the word "babbitt" has come to mean a businessman who adheres too strictly to the social and ethical standards of his group. To say that Lewis felt strongly about a writer's duty to challenge what he sees and disagrees with is to put it mildly. In 1926 he turned down America's coveted Pulitzer prize for literature, saying, "Every compulsion is put upon writers to become safe, polite, obedient ... In protest I must decline the Pulitzer prize."

Unalterably American

In spite of Lewis' continual questioning of the various qualities that he found and disliked in American society, no thoughtful reader of his books can fail to see that he loved the United States, as he loved the town of Gopher Prairie, where *Main Street* takes place. In 1951, when he was dying in Rome, alone in a nursing home with only a nun at his side, he asked that his ashes be sent to his home town. At the simple burial service, a schoolmate of his read from a piece that Lewis had written for the fiftieth anniversary of his high school graduation. It described his home town of Sauk Centre and it ended with "it was a good time, a good place, and a good preparation for life."

Although Lewis felt this way about his birthplace, the people of the town did not at first feel the same way about him, thinking that he had pictured them unfairly in his novel. They have since changed their minds. The year 1960 was Sinclair Lewis Year in Minnesota and the people of Sauk Centre have renamed both an avenue and a park in honor of their famous author-citizen.

Solid Fame

But Lewis' fame is in no way restricted to one town or one state. He is recognized as one of America's foremost authors. Several of his novels have been made into successful motion pictures. In the words of his biographer, "It is impossible to imagine modern American literature without him."

Lewis' former wife sums up the author's importance to the literary history of the United States in the words she wrote upon visiting his grave during a tribute to him held in 1960:

"Even in life he was fully alive only in his writing. He lives in public libraries from Maine to California. . . . He survives in every college and university library. . . . He is an ~~ineradicable~~ part of American cultural history in the twenties and thirties, and no one seeking to recapture and record the habits, frames of mind, social movements, speech, aspírations, admirations, radicalisms, reactions, crusades, and Gargantuan absurdities of the American *demos* during those twenty years will be able to do without him."

—Bibliography—

PRINCIPAL WORKS: *Main Street*, 1920; *Babbitt*, 1922; *Arrowsmith*, 1925; *Elmer Gantry*, 1927; *Dodsworth*, 1929; *It Can't Happen Here*, 1935; *Cass Timberlane*, 1945; *Kingsblood Royal*, 1947; *World So Wide*, 1951.

CARL SANDBURG (1878–1967)

Poet and Lincoln Biographer

SPRINKLED throughout history are men who have had great faith in the wisdom and goodness of the human race. Such a man was Carl Sandburg, son of Swedish immigrants, poet, and writer of one of the great books of modern times—the six-volume biography of Abraham Lincoln.

Born in Poor Family

Sandburg was born on January 6, 1878 in a poor family of nine children in the prairie town of Galesburg, Illinois. His father worked long hours for a railroad company while his mother cooked and baked, washed and mended. Young Sandburg left school when he was thirteen years old to work and contribute to his family's earnings. He delivered newspapers, drove a milkwagon, was a porter in a barber shop. In his late teens he rode a freight train to the West, working

51

in wheat fields in Kansas and washing dishes in hotels in Wyoming and Nebraska.

Tiring of the life of a wanderer, he drifted back to Galesburg and became a house painter, but when in 1898 the Spanish-American War came along, Sandburg at twenty enlisted and served for eight months in Puerto Rico. While in the Army he became friendly with a student at Lombard College in Galesburg, and although Sandburg did not appear to have much interest in getting a formal education, his friend persuaded Sandburg to return to Lombard with him. Sandburg worked his way for the following full four years, but was never graduated. After he became famous, Lombard awarded Sandburg an honorary Doctor of Literature degree.

Worked in Milwaukee

After leaving college, Sandburg went to Milwaukee where he got a job on a newspaper and married Lillian Steichen. He served as secretary to the Mayor of Milwaukee in 1910–12, then moved on to Chicago as associate editor of *System* magazine. Meanwhile, Sandburg had begun writing verse, submitting some to Harriet Monroe who had just started *Poetry, A Magazine of Verse*. In 1914, Sandburg won the magazine's Levinson prize for his poem "Chicago." His first book of verse, *Chicago Poems*, published in 1916, revealed a rambly, vigorous, Whitmanesque style well suited to the Chicago of that day, known principally as "The Hog Butcher of the World."

Sandburg worked for a time in Chicago as an editorial writer on the Chicago *Daily News*, leaving the paper in 1918 to become a war correspondent in Stockholm. After World War I ended, he returned to the United States, settling in Harbert, Michigan, sixty miles from Chicago. It was there that he began writing his monumental biography of Lincoln, his typewriter perched on an apple crate in the attic. The project occupied him for almost fifteen years. Meanwhile, he supported himself by sales of his earlier books and by lectures and readings of his poems. The first two volumes, *Abraham Lincoln: The Prairie Years*, were published in 1926 and the last four, *Abraham Lincoln: The War Years*, in 1939. The work was immediately acclaimed as one of the great biographies of modern times.

Lived in Lincoln Country

It was not at all by coincidence that the idea came to Sandburg to write about Lincoln. He had been brought up in Lincoln country. Across the street from one of Galesburg's schools was a house where Lincoln had stayed as a guest in 1858. Lincoln's home in Springfield, Illinois, was only about one hundred miles away. Many of the men and women of Galesburg had seen or talked with the tall, thoughtful Civil War President who opposed slavery and held the American states together during their most critical time.

Asked on one occasion what prompted his great interest in the Civil War President, Sandburg said, "I wanted to take Lincoln away from the religious bigots and the professional politicians and restore him to the common people to whom he belongs."

The Congress of the United States, recognizing Sandburg

as America's foremost authority on Lincoln, invited the poet-biographer to address the legislators in joint session on February 12, 1959, the 150th anniversary of Lincoln's birth. The distinguished audience, which included not only congressmen but also justices of the Supreme Court, Cabinet members, diplomats and other distinguished guests, heard and were held in the spell of history as Sandburg told about Lincoln's life and time.

Speaking of Lincoln, Sandburg told his audience, "not often in the story of mankind does a man arrive on earth who is both steel and velvet, who is as hard as rock and as soft as drifting fog, who holds in his heart and mind the paradox of terrible storm and peace unspeakable and perfect. . . .

"Democracy? We cannot exactly say what it is," Sandburg continued, "but he [Lincoln] had it. In his blood and bones he carried it. In the breath of his speeches and writings it is there. . . . It was there in the lights and shadows of his personality, a mystery that can be lived but never fully spoken in words."

Sandburg was so successful in recreating Lincoln because he had much in common with Lincoln. Both became deeply convinced of man's dignity as an individual and his place in the whole family of mankind.

Lived in North Carolina

From 1945 until his death in 1967, Sandburg lived in the mountains of western North Carolina. Even at the age of eighty-nine, he wrote several hours each day (or night), in a workroom stuffed with bookshelves and orange crates piled high with hundreds of books and papers about Lincoln. Although age reduced his working schedule, he kept busy, and his lean frame remained strong. His sharp blue eyes looked out on the world between falling locks of straight white hair which was cut only when it began to interfere with his vision. Sandburg was not handsome—his ears were large and his mouth was wide, his cheekbones high—but his face showed a force of character and an awareness that transcended homeliness.

Once he interrupted his quiet schedule to go to Hollywood to collaborate with an old friend, George Stevens, on a movie script about Christ, "The Greatest Story Ever Told." After completing the script, he returned to his North Carolina mountain home.

Asked his formula for his own personal success, Sandburg once said: "It is to be out of jail, to eat and sleep regular. To get what I write printed in a free country for free people. To have a little love in the home and esteem outside the home."

Summing up his long life of struggle and defeat as well as triumph, Sandburg said: "I marvel that I am ambulant and in my right mind as an octogenarian. . . . I have spent as strenuous a life as any man, surviving three wars and two major depressions, but never, not for a moment, did I lose faith in America's future. Time and again I saw the faces of men and women torn and shaken in turmoil, chaos and storm. In each major crisis I have seen despair on the faces of many who struggled to accomplish democratic ideals but happily for the world, their ideas often prevailed. I see great days ahead for men of will and wisdom."

—Bibliography—

PRINCIPAL WORKS: *Chicago Poems*, 1916; *Cornhuskers*, 1918; *Smoke and Steel*, 1920; *Slabs of the Sunburnt West*, 1922; *Abraham Lincoln: The Prairie Years*, 1926; *The American Songbag*, 1927; *The People, Yes*, 1936; *Abraham Lincoln: The War Years*, 1939; *Complete Poems*, 1950.

JOHN P. MARQUAND (1893–1960)

New England Novelist

FUTURE historians searching through dusty libraries to see what life in America was like in the 20th century, may well pause at the name of John P. Marquand, New England novelist, social historian of extraordinary competence, and master of broad satire. Marquand, who is best known for his studies of New England life, died in 1960 at the age of sixty-seven with thirty novels to his credit, as well as numerous articles and short stories.

Literary fame for Marquand, as for many another author, did not come easily. After serving an apprenticeship of almost twenty years as a writer of popular magazine fiction, Marquand at the age of forty-four produced a novel, *The Late George Apley*, about an aristocratic Bostonian—a snob living on fashionable Beacon Hill, stubbornly resisting change. The novel was immediately acclaimed by critics and the public as a brilliant satire of staid old New England aristocracy. Other books in the same vein followed, and Marquand came to be portraying the foibles of the fashionable world he lived in—urbane, smug, self-satisfied, and always a little afraid of not doing the "right" thing.

The Man Marquand

Although born in Wilmington, Delaware in 1893, Marquand spent much of his childhood on the family estate at Newburyport, Massachusetts, near Boston. It was there that his aunt, Margaret Fuller Marquand, of famed New England stock, introduced him to the world of snobbery and tradition-bound life which was typical of New England at the turn of the century. Much of his early background is reflected in his novels.

Like the sons of other upper-class Bostonians—and like his father and grandfather before him—John P. Marquand was duly enrolled at Harvard University. The family fortune, however, had been lost through poor investments, and Marquand became a scholarship student, which made him ineligible for membership in the "best" fraternities.

Forced to seek outside work to help pay his way through college, he found a job on the staff of the *Boston Transcript* and it was there that he began to show the talent which was to bring him fame in later years. After graduation in 1915, Marquand worked as a reporter on the *New York Tribune*, but after several months, quit to join the expeditionary forces of General John J. Pershing, stationed on the Mexican border. When World War I broke out in Europe, Marquand followed Pershing there and rose to the rank of lieutenant. When the war ended, he embarked once again upon a writing career, working for a New York advertising agency. But, at the end of a few months, he became disillusioned and began devoting his full time to writing for popular magazines.

Mystery Stories

Marquand's first published work, a mystery story titled "The Unspeakable Gentleman," appeared in one of America's leading magazines, *The Ladies Home Journal*, in 1922. The profits realized from this and other popular stories were spent by Marquand on a trip to the Orient. Shortly after his return to America, he began writing his "Mr. Moto" stories, a series centered on a Japanese detective. He was paid the top prevailing prices for these stories, which were widely read, but the proceeds still were hardly sufficient to maintain the Marquand family at their fashionable Boston residence and he decided to devote himself to more serious literature. The result was *The Late George Apley*, which won him the Pulitzer prize, one of America's top literary honors.

The characteristics found in George Apley, the hero of Marquand's best-known work, also predominate in other male heroes of his novels. Apley was born at the summit of a formidable Boston pyramid of classes. The novel shows us the warping of Apley's character by the forces of property and position. We see him lose both his early struggle for independence and the Irish girl he wants to marry, and we see him settle down to civic duties and the arid satisfaction of denouncing a new world. Yet for all his bitter prejudices, Apley remains a man of courage and a man of heart. His defeat is brought about by a wholly sincere veneration of the past.

Marquand, a blue-blooded New Englander himself, was also conscious of propriety and the sanctity of the past. While satirizing the New England aristocracy's stubborn resistance to change, he was never able to make a real break with the society in which he grew up and whose values and manners he observed so acutely. Critics have said he might have achieved a still higher place in American literature had he not loved so much—loved to the extent that he could not disassociate himself from the very people he ridiculed.

Unimpressed by Fame

While Marquand varied the characters in his novels (his favorites were well-to-do businessmen, bankers, doctors, lawyers, and writers), he wrote pretty much the same story again and again. It is usually the tale of an affluent, half-disillusioned man searching his past trying to unravel his present, to extricate himself from the web in which accident and circumstance have entangled him. A Marquand hero is usually middle-aged, a conformer who, although he hates the rules, knows he must abide by them, for only by following accepted standards of belief and behavior can he function as the kind of human being he wants to be.

Edward Weeks, former editor of the *Atlantic Monthly*, said of Marquand: "A country is fortunate to have a writer of Marquand's magnetism to hold up the mirror to its extravagance and hypocrisy. He wrote as he felt, and in his own conversation he laid about him in talk that those who heard it will long remember. It was fun to watch him as he approached the verge of the preposterous: his pupils would enlarge, his lips seemed to curl in despair, his voice would rise in exasperation until, with a sudden sniff and outthrust of both hands, he pushed the folly away from him and over the cliff."

Marquand never seemed to be much impressed by his fame. Asked once whether he regarded his popularity as only temporary or believed future generations would like to read his novels, he replied that he felt it was foolish to speculate on the lasting quality of his work. Marquand said he believed that when a person is dead, he is "very, very dead intellectually and spiritually."

He added that there was always the possibility, of course, that some historian would come along some day, poke into the dustheap and come up with something in his work which would still interest people.

Marquand wrote hard, and he wrote steadily, polishing his sentences, counting his cadences, and adjusting his writing hours to what he felt was the maximum his energies would support. There is no substitute for hard work and practice if one wants to become a writer, he advised; the writer must have a compulsion to write every day and not just when the spirit moves him. In writing fiction, he said, the beginning and ending are most important. If you know these, the middle will pretty well take care of itself.

John P. Marquand was an author whose destiny compelled him to do only what he could do well. He was an acute and brilliant observer of upper-class manners. He had the sharp eye of the born reporter, the sensitive ear for speech, the gift of creating atmosphere and of projecting social types.

The key to Marquand's life and writings can be found in these remarks: "My thoughts continually return to the place where my ancestors have come from and where I spent most of my childhood. For me, and I am willing to wager for everyone else, the road one takes, no matter how far it goes, leads to a contradictory sort of frustration, because it always leads to accidental beginnings. It always turns toward home."

—Bibliography—

PRINCIPAL WORKS: *The Unspeakable Gentleman*, 1922; *Ming Yellow*, 1934; *Thank You, Mr. Moto*, 1936; *The Late George Apley*, 1937; *Wickford Point*, 1939; *H. H. Pulham, Esq.*, 1941; *So Little Time*, 1943; *B. F's Daughter*, 1946; *Point of No Return*, 1949; *Women and Thomas Harrow*, 1958.

SHERWOOD ANDERSON   (1876–1941)

Voice of Compassion

LATE ONE day in November, 1912, a thirty-six-year-old Ohio paint manufacturer walked out of his office to begin a new life as an author. A few years later, he was to produce one of the classics of American literature: *Winesburg, Ohio*.

The man who scorned material success for the uncertainties of authorship was Sherwood Anderson, whose deeply perceptive books on the alienation of the individual in American life stand today as a monument to the artist striving to escape the constrictions of conventional society.

Until the day he decided to become an author, Anderson's life was a classic success story. Born in Camden, Ohio, on September 13, 1876, the son of a poor, easy-going, garrulous father and a sturdy, inarticulate former housemaid, Anderson was recognized in his youth as a "go-getter," the energetic, shrewd type who often makes good in business. He showed no early interest in literature nor any inclination to write.

Worked in Chicago

Leaving home in his teens, Anderson worked for awhile at low-paying jobs in Chicago. Then, after serving for a period in the Army, he returned to Ohio and spent a year in a preparatory school, hoping to overcome his scanty education—cut short at fourteen, when he had to leave school to help his parents earn a living. A good student, he was chosen to speak at the graduation ceremony, and so impressed a magazine official in the audience that he was offered a job in the company's advertising department.

Quickly finding his niche in advertising, Anderson became a first-rate copywriter, concocting schemes to part customers from their money and turning out articles in praise of the American businessman. All of this he was later to reject and despise, for already Anderson the idealist had come to regard money-making as a necessary evil.

At the time he abandoned his business career, Anderson was married to a socially established woman, was the father of three children, and headed a prosperous manufacturing concern. Actually, however, he had been leading a double life for years—businessman by day and writer by night. This double existence with its internal conflict between materialism and art had so unnerved Anderson that his health broke down for a brief period after he left the paint company.

He never returned to business life. Instead, he taught for the rest of his life the creed of "anti-success," believing that a life devoted to making money was a wasted life.

Moving to Chicago, he joined a group of writers belonging to the celebrated "Revolt from the Village" movement—among them Theodore Dreiser and Carl Sandburg—and became one of their heroes in 1916 when his first book, *Windy McPherson's Son*, was published. Based primarily on childhood memories of life in a small town, *Windy* deals with the efforts of a young man to break the bonds of stultifying convention.

A year later his second book, *Marching Men*, was published. The hero in this work, infuriated by the misery of his fellow miners, trains vast hordes of workmen to march casually through the streets of Chicago and scare the daylights out of everybody because nobody knew what they were marching for. The miners didn't know, the hero didn't know, and unfortunately Anderson didn't know either! Although hailed by some as graphic and well written, the book was generally regarded as both a commercial and an artistic failure.

"Winesburg"

Between these apprentice novels and the classic *Winesburg, Ohio*, published in 1919, stands no intermediary work indicating a gradual growth of Anderson's talent. *Winesburg* was received with enthusiasm, although one conservative critic labeled it "gutter stuff" because of the sexual irregularities of some of its characters. Anderson received a flood of letters, most of them expressing gratitude in one way or another for writing of the buried aspirations of the American people. Anderson himself described his characters as "grotesques," and actually the two dozen central figures in the book are hardly characters in the usual sense. They are not shown in depth or breadth, complexity or ambiguity. They are allowed no variation of action or opinion. They do not, with the exception of the book's "hero," George Willard, grow or decline. Anderson did not try to represent the surface of life, but drew deliberately distorted, extreme situations. And for that purpose fully rounded characters could only be a complicating blemish.

The figures of *Winesburg* personify to excess a condition of psychic deformity which is the consequence of some crucial failure in their lives—some aborted effort to extend their personalities or proffer their love.

An episodic novel containing loosely bound but closely related sketches, *Winesburg* depends less on dramatic action than on climactic insight for its impact. The story of the God-obsessed minister, for instance, who is a compulsive peeping Tom, reaches its most dramatic point when he breaks the window of his church to spy on a woman who is undressing. Other episodes deal with a mother who is unable to express her love for her son, a woman-hating man with an unfaithful wife, and a frustrated teacher.

Tender Inclusiveness

Winesburg offers no solutions, but there is a tone of tender inclusiveness in the book; Anderson does not mock his characters for their inadequacies. One critic observed that while many American authors besides Anderson have written of the loss of love in the modern world, "few have so thoroughly realized it in the accents of love."

Winesburg, like many of his other works, reflects the world that formed the basic patterns of Anderson's character— small-town Ohio of the 1880's. It was a world not merely western, but a mixture of all those social atmospheres called eastern and western, urban and rural, industrial and handicraft. America was making the transition from an agrarian to an industrial society, and as a point of vantage for the observer of this portion of American history, neither the city nor the farm was so rewarding as the small town. It was this background and the author's own sensitive reaction that produced *Winesburg*, and won for Sherwood Anderson a permanent place in American literature.

Anderson was to return to small-town life. In 1925, he settled in the town of Marion, Virginia, where he continued to turn out books and was also editor of both of the town's two weekly newspapers—one Democratic and one Republican. He died in 1941 while on a tour of South America.

America's D. H. Lawrence

Edward Wagenknecht and other critics have called Anderson "the D. H. Lawrence of American literature." With Lawrence, Anderson shared his revolt against industrialized civilization, and his feeling that in order to recover mental and spiritual health men must learn to live more "natural" lives. From this follows naturally the affection both writers feel for animals, for the primitive, for men who work with their hands, and for nonintellectual types in general.

Anderson wrote several novels dealing directly with the idea of finding a more natural and instinctive life through sex, the most successful of which was *Dark Laughter*, a tale of a newspaperman who walks out on his frigid wife and has an affair with another man's wife. But his other novels along this line were failures, chiefly because he lacked Lawrence's penetrating insights and techniques of constructing a novel.

But the concern with instinctive feeling that he shared with Lawrence came through strongly in Anderson's short stories, which were characterized by intense perception and dominated by instinct rather than ideas.

Bardic Style

Wagenknecht observed that not only Anderson's faults, but his virtues as well, made it difficult for him to write a successful novel. He was at his best in the burning, vivid realization of the moment in such short stories as "I Want to Know Why," "The Egg," and "Death in the Woods," where his seemingly artless bardic style, simulating oral storytelling, was so intimate and effective.

It is in his short stories that he reached that strain of lyrical and nostalgic feeling unequaled by any other American writer. At his best, Anderson creates a world of authentic sentiment in sharp contrast to the toughness of Ernest Hemingway, Norman Mailer, James Jones, and a number of other 20th-century writers who have tended toward an aggressive scorn of the mind, and a fearful retreat from direct emotion.

By comparison Anderson's work seems almost anachronistic, for no one can deny that the world of today is closer to Hemingway and other novelists shaped by his manner than to Anderson. What can we make today of a writer like Anderson in whom there often ran a love for all living things, and who wept when he first saw Paris because "I never thought anything could be so beautiful"? But surely there is a place for Sherwood Anderson, for almost alone among modern writers, he spoke with the voice of compassion.

—Bibliography—

PRINCIPAL WORKS: *Windy McPherson's Son*, 1916; *Marching Men*, 1917; *Winesburg, Ohio*, 1919; *Horses and Men*, 1923; *Dark Laughter*, 1925; *Tar: A Midwest Childhood*, 1926; *Sherwood Anderson's Memoirs*, 1942.

UPTON SINCLAIR (1878–1968)

The Power of a Courageous Pen

ON SEPTEMBER 20, 1904, an ambitious young American novelist arrived in Chicago and put up in a small room at the Stockyards Hotel, located in the heart of the city's meat-packing district. He soon discovered he could go anywhere in the immense packing plants by the simple device of wearing old clothes—he possessed no others—and carrying a workman's lunch pail. In the evenings he sat in workers' homes, asking questions and filling notebooks with what they told him.

It wasn't curiosity that prompted the young writer to explore Chicago's vast meat-packing industry; Upton Sinclair was gathering material for a book to expose conditions which he felt were against the best interests of the United States.

Sinclair wrote his novel and called it *The Jungle*. The

result was explosive. *The Jungle* laid bare the unsanitary practices and unfair working conditions then existing in the meat-packing industry. President Theodore Roosevelt read the book, was greatly impressed, and ordered a federal investigation. The investigation supported the facts presented in Sinclair's novel and resulted in the passage of one of America's most highly prized pieces of legislation, The Pure Food and Drug Act of 1906, the cornerstone of modern American sanitation.

Best Seller

The Jungle quickly became a best seller and was translated into seventeen languages. One of America's most influential newspapers of that day, *The New York Evening World,* wrote that "not in a long time has there been such an example of world-wide fame won in a single day by a book as has come to Upton Sinclair."

Upton Sinclair was born in Baltimore, Maryland, on September 20, 1878, into an unsuccessful branch of a wealthy old Southern family. His father, a liquor salesman, unfortunately drank too much of his own wares and, unable to support his family in Baltimore, he moved to New York where he died an alcoholic.

Young Upton didn't enter school until he was ten years old but he quickly proved himself a child prodigy, completing the first eight grades in less than two years. He entered City College of New York in 1892 at the age of fourteen, and although he won a bachelor's degree he didn't bother to attend the graduation ceremony. While in college, he had begun to write stories and at the age of seventeen he was earning a living for himself and his mother with his pen.

Studied at Columbia

Soon, however, he discovered the need for more education and enrolled in the graduate school at Columbia University, majoring in literature and philosophy. In his autobiography, published in 1962, Sinclair described his work schedule during this three-year period: "I kept two stenographers working all the time taking dictation one day and transcribing the next," he wrote. "In the afternoon I would dictate for about three hours, as fast as I could talk; in the evening I would revise the copy that had been brought in from the previous day, and then take a long walk and think up the incidents for my next day's stint. That left me mornings to attend lectures at Columbia University and to practice the violin."

During his Columbia days, he wrote mainly dime novels and popular romances, but in his early twenties he decided to abandon popular fiction and write a serious novel. The next six years were a period of bitter struggle for Upton Sinclair and the girl he married at the age of twenty-two. Although he wrote five novels during this period, he found little demand for his writing and his earnings were scarcely enough to provide the necessities of life. Then in 1906 came *The Jungle* and world-wide fame.

Prolific Writer

Sinclair took the money he made from *The Jungle* and put it into a Utopian experiment in New Jersey. There he gathered a small community of writers and their families around him, planning to share with them the burdens of housekeeping and child care. Disaster soon struck. The cooperative dwelling where the writers lived burned down after a year and most of Sinclair's money went up in smoke with it.

In 1915, after a period of travel, Sinclair settled in California. The next few years he published *Upton Sinclair's Magazine,* meanwhile continuing to write novels. During the period from 1917–40 he wrote about many areas of contemporary American life, from oil fields to coal mines to big-city newspaper offices. The novels all dealt with the same theme as *The Jungle,* the theme of social reform.

Candidate for Governor

In 1934 Upton Sinclair ran for governor of California on the Democratic ticket, promising wide social reforms if elected. Although he lost the election, he attracted the highest vote that had ever been given a Democratic candidate for governor in California.

Sinclair clearly was more of a writer than a politician, and with the publication of *World's End* in 1940, he introduced a series of novels built around world events occuring between 1940 and 1953. The series is tied together by a character named Lanny Budd, a young man who travels far and wide and usually happens to be in the right spot at the right time. In 1943, one of this series of novels, *Dragon's Teeth,* earned the Pulitzer prize.

Contemporary Historian

A good friend of Sinclair's, George Bernard Shaw, once said that when people asked him what had happened during his long lifetime, he referred them not to the newspaper files but to Sinclair's novels. Sinclair, indeed, was a superb journalist and his books comprise a significant record of

20th-century American culture. But he was far more than a chronicler of his time. He was also a fine storyteller. Sir Arthur Conan Doyle, the English writer who created Sherlock Holmes, considered him one of the greatest novelists in the world. Sinclair told his story as he saw it, and for the good of humanity. His books were written with the immediate purpose of helping mankind and throughout his lifetime he was a fearless and untiring crusader.

"If I was not always right," he said, "I was looking for the right. What more can a man do with his life?"

—Bibliography—

PRINCIPAL WORKS: *The Jungle*, 1906; *King Coal*, 1917; *The Brass Check*, 1919; *Oil!*, 1927; *Money Writes*, 1927; *American Outpost*, 1932; *Lanny Budd Series—World's End*, 1940; *Between Two Worlds*, 1941; *Dragon's Teeth*, 1942; *Wide Is the Gate*, 1943; *Presidential Agent*, 1944; *Dragon's Harvest*, 1945; *A World to Win*, 1946; *Presidential Mission*, 1947; *One Clear Call*, 1948; *O Shepherd Speak!*, 1949; *Return of Lanny Budd*, 1953.

EUGENE O'NEILL (1888–1953)

The Delights of Tragedy

OF AMERICA's 20th-century writers, none perhaps has plumbed to such depths of despair or endured such personal tragedy as Eugene O'Neill, the most widely translated dramatist in the world today with the possible exception of Shakespeare and Bernard Shaw.

O'Neill once wrote: "I don't think any real dramatic stuff is created out of the top of your head . . . I have never written anything which did not come directly or indirectly from some event or impression of my own."

O'Neill had a wealth of personal experience—much of it anguish, frustration, and tragedy—to draw upon, and it is no wonder that most of his work is a dark and brooding interpretation of a world which he described as "a gorgeously ironical, beautifully indifferent, splendidly suffering bit of chaos."

Wrote about Family

In his last and perhaps his greatest play, *Long Day's Journey into Night,* O'Neill wrote about a family called the Tyrones; but the real people behind the characters in the drama were his own family—his parents, his brother, and himself—whom he portrayed with remorseless, blinding honesty.

The mother in the play is a drug addict. The father is a swaggering miser, an embittered actor who wanted to play the classics but instead spent twenty years portraying the role of the "Count of Monte Cristo," a sickeningly sentimental but popular and profitable melodrama. The elder brother is a cynical, weak-willed drunkard, and the younger brother is racked by sickness and a tormented soul.

These are the characters in the play; but they run true to their real-life prototypes—the O'Neill family itself. Eugene O'Neill's father died in 1920, a disappointed old man filled with self-pity over failure to reach greatness on the stage. The elder brother, Jamie, died three years later of alcoholism. Eugene's mother alone managed to reverse the grim pattern of the O'Neills. She entered a Catholic convent, overcame her addiction to dope, and died peacefully in 1922.

Young Eugene O'Neill, the future playwright, had been bruised too badly by his dismal and tragic youth to come out unscathed. He took refuge in drink, and in middle age, after achieving fame as a dramatist, became afflicted with a palsy which at times was so violent that he couldn't hold a pencil. Miserable and despondent, he often threatened suicide but was unable to summon sufficient courage. With advancing years, he began to inflict his pent-up torment on his children, whom he seemed to resent for disturbing his privacy and interfering with his work.

O'Neill abandoned his first wife while she was pregnant and didn't see his first son, Eugene, Jr., until he was twelve and only rarely after that. After drinking a bottle of whisky, Eugene, Jr., committed suicide in 1950. Eugene O'Neill's other two children, Shane and Oona, fared little better. Rebuffed by his father, Shane began taking dope while serving as a merchant seaman in World War II and has been frequently arrested in subsequent years. When the dramatist's daughter, Oona, in whom he had only showed casual interest, married famed movie star Charlie Chaplin at the age of 18, O'Neill fairly exploded with paternal wrath. At his death in 1953, O'Neill disinherited both Shane and Oona.

Wandering Youth

Born in a hotel room in New York City on October 16, 1888, O'Neill spent most of his first seven years traveling about America with his actor-father. His early education was received mostly at Catholic boarding schools. He entered Princeton University in 1906 but was suspended at the end of his freshman year for misconduct and never returned. During the next few years he prospected unsuccessfully for gold in Honduras, sailed on ships bound for South America, frequented tough saloons on New York's waterfront and worked as a newspaper reporter in New London, Connecticut. In 1912 he was stricken with tuberculosis, after which he began to write plays, achieving his first big success with *Beyond the Horizon* which won him the Pulitzer prize in 1920. He was to receive the same award twice more—in 1922 for *Anna Christie* and in 1928 for *Strange Interlude*. In 1918, after divorcing his first wife, he married again, but in 1929 deserted his second wife and their two children to marry a glamorous actress, Carlotta Monterey. A strong-willed woman, Carlotta tried to exert a stabilizing influence on O'Neill's life but without much success. Their years together were changeable and hectic. A virtual invalid, O'Neill died of bronchial pneumonia at the age of sixty-five in a Boston hotel room.

Following O'Neill's death, interest and critical acclaim for his work declined; but in recent years, with the posthumous Broadway production of *Long Day's Journey into Night* and the revival of many of his other plays, he has come to be recognized as one of the world's great 20th-century dramatists.

Sense of Tragedy

What is the quality which is uniquely O'Neill's among modern American playwrights? What is it about his plays that has won him a solid international reputation? The word which perhaps best describes the essence of his greatness is tragedy: tragedy which Aristotle defined as the story of a noble man, neither villainous nor perfectly virtuous, who is defeated but not wholly subdued by something too large for him to cope with. Such a story, Aristotle thought, could be recognized by its effect, which is to "purge the soul by pity and terror." The hero of such a tragedy, the Greek philosopher believed, cannot be "a little man." He must represent the nobility of purpose of which human nature is capable. We may pity him but that pity must be for strength defeated, not for weakness. O'Neill has come closer than any other American dramatist to approximating this Aristotelian concept of tragedy.

Believed in Man

During his thirty years of creative effort, O'Neill often expressed his theories of drama and his vision of what it should be. In much of this comment, his deep sense of the tragic is spelled out. "The tragedy of life," he once wrote, "gives Man a tremendous significance, but without his losing fight with fate he would be a tepid, silly animal. I say 'losing fight' only symbolically, for the brave individual always wins. Fate can never conquer his or her spirit . . ."

On another occasion, O'Neill wrote: "I have an innate feeling of exultance about tragedy, which comes from the Greek feeling for tragedy. The tragedy of Man is perhaps the only significant thing about him."

At another time, he said: "I'll write about happiness if I ever happen to meet up with that luxury and find it sufficiently dramatic and in harmony with any deep rhythm of life. . . . I know there is more of it [happiness] in one real tragedy than in all the happy-ending plays ever written."

Paradoxically, there is hope and tonic in O'Neill's tragedies just as in those of Shakespeare and Sophocles. In his plays the human spirit remains unconquered—man believes in himself if in nothing else. Perhaps this accounts for O'Neill's high position today in world drama.

Granville Hicks, American critic, in an article called "From a Black Abyss, a Man and Artist," in *The Saturday Review* of April 7, 1962, summed up O'Neill's career as a man and dramatist in these words:

"He was in many ways anything but an admirable man.

. . . We see the debauchery of the early years, his callousness toward his children, his arbitrariness and vanity. His destructive impulses, turned primarily against himself, were sometimes turned against others, and he wrought more than his share of evil. Yet in his devotion to his art he was an heroic figure, and it was this devotion that saved him as it has saved many another artist. In his terrible last years— terrible because of incapacitating disease and because of a series of tragic blows that went beyond anything in his plays —he displayed a splendid dignity. . . . O'Neill lived in his abyss and made it his home. That was his triumph as a dramatist and as a man.

"Although O'Neill's reputation is much higher than it was a decade ago, there is still plenty of dissent. His denigrators always point out that, whatever his virtues, he lacked greatness of language, and most of his admirers concede the point. Even O'Neill himself knew he was not the poet he wanted and needed to be. As a result it is a disappointment to read his plays; but to see them is, in spite of this failing, an extraordinary experience. Not many dramatists in all of literary history have been able to lay so strong a spell upon their audiences."

—Bibliography—

PRINCIPAL WORKS: *Beyond the Horizon,* 1920; *The Emperor Jones,* 1921; *Anna Christie,* 1923; *Desire under the Elms,* 1925; *The Great God Brown,* 1926; *Lazarus Laughed,* 1927; *Mourning Becomes Electra,* 1931; *Ah, Wilderness!,* 1933; *Long Day's Journey into Night,* 1956.

THOMAS WOLFE (1900–1937)

"Millionaire of Words"

THOMAS WOLFE, a hulking, slow-moving giant of a man conscious of standing "six-foot-six in a world of five-foot-eight"—came close to creating the "Great American Novel" that critics have dreamed of—a work epitomizing the life, spirit, and character of the United States. Living on canned beans, coffee, and cigarettes, working by day and writing by night, Wolfe captured the essence of a cross section of America, drawing from the experience of his own lonely life to write one of the classics of modern American literature, *Look Homeward, Angel.*

Although *Look Homeward, Angel* purports to be a novel, it is in fact a thinly veiled autobiography of Thomas Wolfe's unhappy boyhood in his native city of Asheville, North Carolina. It is also the story of Wolfe's violent-tempered father and shrewd, tight-fisted mother, who were separated when Tom was seven years old. Wolfe also portrayed in *Look Homeward, Angel* other relatives, friends, and acquaintances who lived in his home town—all painted larger than life, their characters laid bare for all to see.

Home Town Angered

It was only natural, therefore, when Wolfe's novel was published in 1929, that the people of his home town would be furious. Asheville was known then, as it is today, as a picturesque, peaceful mountain resort. Many of its citizens feared that the "bad publicity" Wolfe had given the famed resort would hurt its business. Some wrote to Wolfe, threatening to kill him if he ever came home. One old lady who had known Wolfe all his life, wrote him she would like to see his "big overgroan karkus [overgrown carcass] dragged across the public square."

Wolfe had anticipated the storm of protest over publication of *Look Homeward, Angel* and tried to soften it in a foreword. The book, he said, "was written in innocence and nakedness of spirit. We are," he added, "the sum of all the moments of our lives . . . and if the writer has used the clay of life to make his book, he has only used what all men must."

If Wolfe's *Look Homeward, Angel* was nothing less than life itself, it can be said of him that through his rich literary gift he was able to transform relatives, friends, and acquaintances into a great gallery of portraits, each finely modeled and shaded. What makes the book great, however, is Wolfe's success in using people and situations to illuminate fundamental truths. In the Gant household about which Wolfe wrote, the evil that pervades the family and warps the lives of all who came in contact with it, is selfishness. Love might have dispelled the evil, but each Gant was too busy with his own affairs to look into the hearts of others.

Laced with Poetry

Look Homeward, Angel is laced with fine poetry. Here is Wolfe's description of a day in summer: "The day was like gold and sapphires: there was a swift slash and sparkle, intangible and multifarious, like sunlight on roughened water, all over the land. A rich warm wind was blowing, turning all the leaves back the same way, and making mellow music through all the lute strings of flower and grass and fruit. . . . A dog bayed faintly in the cove, his howl spent and broken by the wind. A cowbell tinkled gustily. In the thick wood below them the rich notes of birds fell from their throats, straight down, like nuggets. . . ."

Thomas Wolfe was born in October 3, 1900, in Asheville, North Carolina, the son of W. O. Wolfe, a stonecutter, and Eliza Wolfe, who ran a boardinghouse. After his father and mother separated, Tom lived with his mother and five brothers and sisters, but the broken family affected him deeply. Years later he wrote of the loneliness and terror of his childhood, when he felt himself groping desperately toward light and life.

Escape into Books

Wolfe retreated from his unhappy life into the world of books; before he was twelve had read Shakespeare's works, *The Harvard Classics,* and was familiar with the novels of Thackeray and other standard English novelists and poets. At fifteen he entered the University of North Carolina, where he seems to have been able to slough off his boyhood despondency, participating actively in college affairs, editing the school newspaper and finding time to write plays, one of which, "The Return of Buck Gavin," was published. World War I interrupted his schooling, but after the armistice he graduated from Carolina and moved on to Harvard University, where he studied drama under the late Dr. George Pierce Baker, famed for his "English 47" playwrighting course.

After receiving his Master of Arts degree at Harvard, Wolfe taught English at New York University but, growing restless, he sailed for England where he started work on his first novel. Returning to New York, he taught by day at the University, writing by night until *Look Homeward, Angel*, which ran to 250,000 words, was ready for submission to publishers. Several publishers rejected it before one of America's biggest houses, Scribner's, decided in 1929 to bring it out.

Other Novels

Encouraged by the success of *Look Homeward, Angel*, Wolfe conceived the dream of putting the whole of America into a single work in the form of three gigantic novels. During the next eight years, wandering about Europe and living at times in America, Wolfe wrote *Of Time and the River*, *The Web and the Rock*, and *You Can't Go Home Again*—the last two of which were not published until soon after his death. He gave promise of going on to still greater heights, but driving himself brutally to say all he had to say "within the bitter briefness of man's days," he undermined his health, dying at the age of thirty-seven of complications following an attack of pneumonia.

Torrent of Words

Everything that Wolfe thought or felt or feared or hoped, he wanted to put on paper. He wanted to pour out everything he remembered in one torrential flood of words, but he also wanted to increase his reservoir of memories by going everywhere and doing everything. He wanted to devour the whole world with his mind—persons, books, landscapes, joys, sorrows—and then digest it into written words.

Writing about Wolfe's determination to wring from his life every ounce of creative energy before death overtook him, William Faulkner said: "Man has but one short life to write in, and there is so much to be said, and of course he wants to say it all before he dies. My admiration for Wolfe is that he tried his best to get it all said: he was willing to throw away style, coherence, all the rules of preciseness, to try to put all the experience of the human heart on the head of a pin, as it were. He may have had the best talent of us all, he may have been the greatest American writer if he had lived longer. . . ."

—Bibliography—

PRINCIPAL WORKS: *Look Homeward, Angel,* 1929; *Of Time and the River,* 1935; *The Story of a Novel,* 1936; *The Web and the Rock,* 1939; *You Can't Go Home Again,* 1940; *The Hills Beyond,* 1941; *Letters to His Mother,* 1943.

WALLACE STEVENS (1879–1955)

Businessman Poet

MOST BUSINESSMEN are portrayed as realistic, down-to-earth men who spend their life and talent trying to make money. There are exceptions, of course—one of the most outstanding in recent years being Wallace Stevens, who, while holding a high position in an American insurance company, won world-wide recognition as a poet.

Stevens was born in Reading, Pennsylvania, in 1879, just two hundred years after his ancestors, who were of German-Dutch origin, came to America to escape religious persecution. Young Stevens went to Harvard University where he wrote some poetry but concentrated on preparing himself for a law career. After graduating, he began practicing law in New York City but managed to find time occasionally to visit old college friends who were painting and writing in

Greenwich Village, the city's art center, thus maintaining his interest in poetry.

Lawyer-Poet

Stevens first attracted the attention of literary critics in 1914 with the publication of a few poems in *Poetry* magazine. His first book of poems, *Harmonium*, appeared in 1923. It seems incredible, one critic said, that a man like Stevens, who spent his time delving into the intricacies of legal matters, could write delicate, imaginative poetry full of many references to painting, sculpture, music, and faraway places.

As the years passed, Wallace Stevens continued his dual role of businessman-poet, gaining increasing stature in both. From 1916 he had been associated with one of America's largest insurance companies, the Hartford Accident and Indemnity Company of Connecticut, starting in the legal department. In 1934, the company recognized his great talent as an insurance lawyer by naming him vice-president of the concern. Despite his increased business responsibilities, Stevens maintained his passion for poetry, usually composing his poems while on long walks in the late afternoon or night.

Discussing the relation between business and the arts, Stevens once said: "It gives man character as a poet to have a daily contact with a job. I doubt whether I've lost a thing by leading an exceedingly regular and disciplined life. Poetry and surety claims are not as unlikely a combination as they seem. There is nothing perfunctory about them, for each case is different."

Role of Poet

To understand Stevens' poems, it is necessary to understand his philosophy and the role of the 20th-century poet. Stevens recognized, first of all, that man lives in a physical world of real things—taxicabs, blackbirds, worms, pineapples, jars. Then, secondly, that man has a faculty which gives him power over these real objects to shape them into things of beauty. For Stevens, even a dump heap could provide material for poetry:

> The wrapper on the can of pears,
> The cat in the paper bag, the corset, the box
> From Esthonia

According to Stevens, it is where man's imagination takes him that is the poet's chief reason for being. The poet's job, he says, is to help us escape, through an enhanced perception, from things as they are to things as they can be. In this respect Stevens has frequently been compared to T. S. Eliot, who is also concerned with the nature of the art of poetry and the role of the poet and artist, particularly in modern society where science dominates.

Stevens' Philosophy

Stevens' poems are often difficult to comprehend even for the highly literate and sophisticated reader because of their intricate abstractions and sudden shifts of metaphor. When Stevens views a flower, he does not see the flower as a simple image, but as a complicated object. He believes that by utilizing the imagination we can make the object that we see more than it is. Hence, Stevens can write a poem about a commonplace blackbird, as a romantic poet might write about a skylark, and he calls that poem "Thirteen Ways of Looking at a Blackbird." Objectively, there is only one way of looking at a blackbird, but imagination makes it possible to see it in thirteen—indeed countless—ways.

"Wallace Stevens is a rhetorician," wrote Howard Baker, poet and teacher, "a persuasive artificer of the poetic line.... His poetry gains part of its loftiness from brilliant epithets and daring images."

Poet of Urban Life

Stevens differs from most other major poets of the 20th century. Typical is his attitude toward the modern metropolis. He does not make the city itself a symbol of moral decay and loss of faith, as Eliot's "The Waste Land." He is conscious of the dirt and crowds and emptiness of cities, but he has an insight that goes deeper. In "Notes Toward a Supreme Fiction," he wrote:

> The truth depends on a walk
>   around a lake.
> A composing as the body tires, a stop
>   to see hepatica. . . .

Stevens, like most poets, rarely wrote on social and political themes, but he rejected, throughout his life, the ideology of the communists, who believe this world can be made perfect through social reform and the dictatorship of the state. Stevens sees a world

> that moves from waste
> To waste, out of the hopeless
>   waste of the past
> Into a hopeful waste to come . . .

and knows that a revolution is just one more aspect of "the ever-never-changing-same."

> The future must bear within it every past,
> Not least the pasts destroyed, magniloquent
> Syllables, pewter on ebony, yet still
> A board for bishops' grapes, the happy form
> That revolution takes for connoisseurs: . . .

Wallace Stevens died on August 2, 1955. It was just ten months earlier, on his seventy-fifth birthday, that he had celebrated the publication of his collected poems—a volume that won both the National Book Award and the Pulitzer prize. His contribution to American literature will long be remembered. Certainly it was a fortunate circumstance for the world of letters that a man of Stevens' imagination found an insurance office a point of vantage for looking at

> things chalked
> On the sidewalk so that the pensive man
> may see.

—Bibliography—

PRINCIPAL WORKS: *Harmonium*, 1923; *The Necessary Angel* (critical essays), 1951; *Collected Poems*, 1954.

WILLIAM CARLOS WILLIAMS
(1883–1963)
Poet and Baby Doctor

THERE WAS a time when poets were considered idlers, living in an ivory tower, composing—when inspiration came—verses which some day might become a part of the world's great literature. Often even the best poets lived precariously, sometimes on the verge of starvation, for the writing of poetry has seldom been a secure way to earn a living.

In the 20th century, however—at least in America—the old concept of the poet as an idealistic dreamer living apart from the world has changed. One of America's finest modern poets, William Carlos Williams, was a man of practical affairs, devoting his life both to poetry and to the practice of medicine.

Baby Doctor

Williams died on March 4, 1963, at the age of seventy-nine, leaving behind him some forty volumes of poetry, short stories, novels, plays, and essays. Critics rate him the equal—in some ways perhaps the superior—of such great American contemporary poets as Robert Frost, Ezra Pound, Wallace Stevens, and E. E. Cummings. The marvel is that Williams, while practicing medicine for forty years and delivering more than two thousand babies, was able to turn out an average of a book a year of distinguished literature. America's highest poetic honor, the Pulitzer prize, was awarded him posthumously.

Williams never felt that his medical practice suffered from his poetry or his poetry from his practice of medicine. "One feeds the other," he said—explaining that medicine got him out among his neighbors, while writing let him express what he had been turning over in his mind as he went along.

Asked once if he didn't get tired of delivering babies and would rather spend more of his time writing poetry, Williams replied: "No. I'm a baby doctor. I take care of babies and try to make them grow. I enjoy it. Nothing is more appropriate to a man than an interest in babies."

Poet of the City

This remarkable poet-physician was born in 1883 in Rutherford, New Jersey—an ugly industrial area, its landscape scarred with gray brick factories, smoking chimneys, and swampy marshland where the rusting hulks of abandoned automobiles and worn-out machinery could often be seen. This hard-bitten, faceless section where he grew up and spent most of his life was, however, grist for Williams' poetic genius. In his most famous poem, "Paterson," a nearby industrial city, he wrote with imagination and beauty about the city's thirsty waterfalls and trees stunted by concrete and grime. He found poetry here, he says, because he felt that poetry "clusters about common things." Williams could see poetry in racing fire trucks, factories, smoking chimneys, even garbage trucks and junk piles.

In his poem "Spring Storm"—with its setting in a dismal city—he saw nature's liberation of pavement and earth as a hint of higher human values:

> The sky has given over
> its bitterness. . . .
>
> Still the snow keeps
> its hold on the ground. . . .
>
> But water, water
> From a thousand runnels!
> It collects swiftly,
> dappled with black
> cuts a way for itself
> through green ice in the gutters. . . .

Mixed Ancestry

William Carlos Williams liked to talk about his mixed ancestry, sometimes referring to himself as a "melting pot of nations." His mother was born in Puerto Rico of French, Spanish, Jewish, and Dutch blood. His father was of English parentage, settling in Rutherford, New Jersey, a few years before William Carlos was born. After completing grammar school, young Williams studied in Switzerland, Paris, and New York, then entered medical school at the University of Pennsylvania, receiving his degree in 1906. He interned in New York, and in Germany, Spain, and Italy, returning to Rutherford in 1910 where he practiced medicine until he suffered a stroke in 1951, seriously impairing his health.

Dr. Williams believed there are no ideas except in things, and all things were treasured by him, both for themselves and for the emotion that lay behind them. It was this attitude toward life, perhaps, that helped him to master the knack of treating poems as patients and patients as poems. "To treat a man as material for a work of art," he once wrote, "makes him somehow come alive for me." It was said of Williams that "no one could love anything as much as he loved everything." Using the material at hand—material many another poet would have shrugged off as too prosaic to write about—Dr. Williams' poems were like snapshots—rough, direct, staccato glimpses of life. Typical of his style—stripped of verbal ornamentation and avoiding personal comment—is the short poem "The Young Housewife":

> At ten A.M., the young housewife
> moves about in negligee behind
> the wooden walls of her husband's house.
>
> I pass solitary in my car.
> Then again she comes to the curb
> to call the ice-man, fish-man and stands
> shy, uncorseted, tucking in
> stray ends of hair, and I compare her
> to a fallen leaf.
>
> The noiseless wheels of my car
> rush with a crackling sound over
> dried leaves as I bow and pass smiling.

Died in the Spring

William Carlos Williams died in the spring—the season when warm winds begin to touch the icy North Atlantic coast of America where he lived. This passage from one of his poems might well serve as his epitaph:

> Spring days
> swift and mutable
> winds blowing four ways
> hot and cold
> shaking the flowers—
>
> Now the northeast wind
> moving in fogs leaves the grass
> cold and dripping. The night
> is dark. But in the night
> the southeast wind approaches.
> The owner of the orchard
> lies in bed
> with open windows
> and throws off his covers
> one by one.

—Bibliography—

PRINCIPAL WORKS: *Poems,* 1909; *Sour Grapes,* 1921; *Spring and All,* 1922; *Paterson,* 1946; *Autobiography,* 1951; *Selected Essays,* 1954; *Selected Letters,* 1957.

E. E. CUMMINGS   (1894–1962)

Poet, Individualist

In 1917 in a French courtroom, a tall, blond young man stood on trial for espionage. A few months before, filled with a youthful idealism and a resolute belief in democracy and the rights of the individual, he had come from America to serve as an ambulance driver with the French Red Cross.

Now, at his trial, the case against him was so flimsy that even the officer in charge was merely going through the motions of an investigation. In the end it all boiled down to one question—"Do you hate the Germans?" The young man had only to answer that he did and the charges would have been dropped.

But Edward Estlin Cummings, who was to become one of America's greatest poets, was a strong individualist. He would not have "hate" put into his mouth by anyone. His reply was only, "I love the French."

But the officer insisted, "Do you hate the Germans?"

Again came the stubborn reply, "I love the French."

The officer had no choice but to sentence him to jail for three months.

Faith in Man's Individuality

This incident clearly established the characteristics that marked E. E. Cummings' life and literary career.

Cummings' lifelong belief was a simple faith in the miracle of man's individuality. Much of his literary effort was directed against what he considered the principal enemies of this individuality—mass thought, group conformity, and commercialism.

In keeping with this view, Cummings advised young poets that "to be nobody-but-yourself—in a world which is doing its best, night and day, to make you somebody else—means to fight the hardest battle which any human being can fight."

Once in a lecture, he further asserted that "If poetry is your goal, you've got to forget all about punishments and all about rewards and all about self-styled obligations and remember one thing only: that it's you—nobody else—who determines your destiny and decides your fate."

Individualist

The principle of individualism which dominated his life may have been acquired in part from his father, a fiercely nonconformist Unitarian minister. Another influence, perhaps, was the area in which young Cummings grew up: New England, famous for its rebellious individualism from the time of the American Revolution.

Born in Cambridge, Massachusetts, on October 14, 1894, Cummings went to high school in his home town and later attended Harvard University, graduating in 1916. Like many other young nonconformists of that World War I period, he enlisted in the Red Cross ambulance service in Europe. After serving three months in prison on the espionage charge, he wrote a novel, *The Enormous Room*, based on his experiences in France. The book was a popular success, and some critics consider it today among the best novels written about World War I.

Cummings' first love, however, was poetry and during the next ten years he wrote five volumes of poems, including one of his most famous volumes, *Tulips and Chimneys*. He did his writing in Paris and New York, shuttling often between the two cities. In both places he spent his time with distinct, out-of-the-ordinary people, artists, and writers noted for their individuality as well as for their talent. In Paris he became acquainted with the expatriate colony of Americans who had come to work and live there, and in New York he settled in Greenwich Village, a section of the city famous for its off-beat characteristics.

Criticized Communism

In 1933 Cummings wrote a travel book, *Eimi*, based on a trip to the Soviet Union. Again expressing his individualism, the book was distinguished not only by its unconventional prose but by its scathing criticism of the communist system, coming at a time when many intellectuals were expressing what amounted to an unfounded sympathy with the communist cause. After this book he again returned to writing poetry, settling for good in New York.

In the spring of 1952 he was invited to give the annual Charles Eliot Norton Lectures in poetry at Harvard. Declaring that he didn't have "the remotest notion of posing as a lecturer," Cummings delivered instead a series of what he called "non-lectures"—witty, casual talks and readings which were later published in book form. A decade later, in September, 1962, Cummings suffered a stroke and died in a hospital near his New Hampshire summer home at the age of sixty-seven.

His Poetry, Expression of Individuality

Cummings' unorthodox poetic style was in itself an expression of his individuality. Often his poems were recklessly strewn with out-of-order syllables, letters, and punctuation marks. He rarely used capital letters and until the mid-1930's preferred his own name to be written in lower case (e.e. cummings).

His poetry contained a wild variety of poetic rhythms—lines that crept, leaped, staggered, paced proudly, or flowed smoothly. A reviewer of his poems has said "he wrote carnival verse, brightly colored and splattered with a thousand sounds, and then he pitched it all over the typographical lot in a frank attempt to grab his reader's eye."

Because he sought out the reader's interest, Cummings for a long time had the reputation of a superficial writer bent merely on shocking the complacency of his readers. Although this was partly the case, it should not obscure his profounder merits. True, he experimented with new forms, unconventional typographical arrangements, oddities of spelling and punctuation, and both technical and wildly impolite language, but the reader who turns a second or third time to his poems discovers that most of his innovations possess a genuine poetic content.

All Aimed Toward Individuality

Cummings' strange typography and punctuation, for example, effectively reinforced or amplified not only his poem's rhythmical structure but also its innermost meaning. His poetic technique was a direct consequence of his point of view—that of an individualist and an enemy of restriction and regimentation.

In one of his "non-lectures" at Harvard he said: "So far as I am concerned, poetry and every other art was, is, and forever will be strictly and distinctly a question of individuality."

Unique Style

Although Cummings' style was unique, his poems frequently contain conventional and recurring themes— love, nature, and an abiding faith in the underdog. In fact, his love poems first brought him fame as a poet. Typical of these earlier poems is this selection from *Tulips and Chimneys*:

> it may not always be so; and i say
> that if your lips, which i have loved, should touch
> another's, and your dear strong fingers clutch
> his heart, as mine in time not far away;
> if on another's face your sweet hair lay
> in such a silence as i know, or such
> great writhing words as, uttering overmuch,
> stand helplessly before the spirit at bay;
> if this should be, i say if this should be—

you of my heart, send me a little word;
that i may go unto him, and take his hands,
saying, Accept all happiness from me.
then shall i turn my face, and hear one bird
sing terribly afar in the lost lands.

Cummings' works were a combination of fine poetic talent, unorthodox style, a good sense of humor, and a large measure of his own individuality. His was an authentic voice, telling us of his beliefs, his life, and his times.

Fellow poet Archibald MacLeish perhaps best sums up E. E. Cummings in these words: "There are very few people who deserve the word poet. Cummings was one of them."

—Bibliography—

PRINCIPAL WORKS: *Tulips and Chimneys*, 1923; *XLI Poems*, 1925; *Is 5*, 1926; *ViVa*, 1931; *No Thanks*, 1935; *Six Non-lectures*, 1953; *Poems*, 1923–1954; *95 Poems*, 1958.

F. SCOTT FITZGERALD   (1896–1940)

"The Roaring Twenties"

SOME AUTHORS enjoy great popularity in their lifetime only to fall into neglect after death. Others are forgotten for a while and then, upon re-examination by readers and critics, are found to possess qualities before unrecognized, and take their place in their nation's literature. Such an author who was "rediscovered" after death is F. Scott Fitzgerald, American novelist, known as the spokesman of America's "Roaring Twenties"—the Jazz Age.

Fitzgerald is best understood against the background of his age—the generation which came to maturity in the United States following World War I. After the terrible butchery of that savage war, American youth wanted to forget, and it found its expression in jazz—the new, lively music which came out of America's South. This new "flaming youth" generation, as it was called, was disillusioned, flippant, hard-boiled. Pleasure-loving, it found the excitement it craved in night clubs, drinking, fast dancing. Scott Fitzgerald was one of these young people. With the publication of his novel *This Side of Paradise* in 1920 at the age of twenty-four, he quickly established himself as the spokesman of what has since come to be known as the "Lost Generation."

"Cracked Plate"

The trouble with Fitzgerald was that his generation grew up. The thirties came with their world-wide depression and most people were too busy making a living to worry or care about the gay life Fitzgerald portrayed. Fitzgerald was never able to quite adjust himself to the new age and, after battling for years against alcoholism, died in 1940 of a heart attack at the age of forty-four. In latter years, he described himself as "a cracked plate."

Although Fitzgerald's life ended unhappily, it had an auspicious beginning. Born in 1896 in the city of St. Paul, Minnesota into a prosperous family of Irish descent, he was given the opportunity of a fine education at Princeton University but failed to graduate. His classmates blamed his academic failure on his "scribbling." He was too fond of writing, they said, to study. After leaving Princeton he joined the U.S. Army, serving as aide-de-camp to General J. A. Ryan until his discharge in 1919, when he went to New York and tried to find a job as a newspaper reporter. Seven papers are said to have refused to employ him.

Best Seller

The press' failure to appreciate his writing talent might

have discouraged many a young author, but not Scott Fitzgerald. He managed to make a living for three months writing advertising slogans for street cars, then sold a short story to *Smart Set*, a leading publication of that period. Elated, he returned to his home in St. Paul to work on his novel *This Side of Paradise*, which was published the following year, rocketing Fitzgerald to prominence in the literary world.

This Side of Paradise was a light, frothy story and quickly became a best seller, not because of any remarkable merit in either the story or the writing but because it was the perfect expression of the world of the postwar American adolescent—the Jazz Age. In fact, Fitzgerald was credited with "inventing his generation," of giving a name to it, of interpreting and guiding it.

Gaiety and Tragedy

The twenty-four-year-old Fitzgerald, a handsome broad-shouldered youth with alert green eyes, welcomed his acclaim as a celebrity and the money it brought. That same year he married Zelda Sayre, a red-haired beauty from the Southern state of Alabama, also a writer, and for the next few years they lived mostly on fashionable Long Island in New York and in Europe—frequently in Rome and on the Riviera, an ideal setting for the fast-living Fitzgeralds. Together with his strikingly beautiful wife, Fitzgerald moved through a world of speakeasies, flappers, and night clubs—drinking heavily, dancing fast, and making merry. Meanwhile, he continued to write, putting on paper what he saw from the point of view of a little boy from America's Midwest "standing outside a fancy ballroom with his nose pressed to the glass, wondering how much the tickets cost and who paid for the music." In 1925, Scott Fitzgerald published what is usually regarded as his finest novel, *The Great Gatsby*, which tells of the rise and fall of a rich New York bootlegger.

But in the years ahead, tragedy was to strike hard at the gay, pleasure-loving Fitzgeralds. Zelda began to act strangely, was pronounced insane and confined to a hospital in Asheville, North Carolina. Desperate over the hopeless condition of his wife, Fitzgerald drank more heavily than ever. Having now outlived the era of the "Roaring Twenties," he felt out of place, lost in the practical, hard-working world of the thirties. A free spender, he had squandered the money earned from his earlier books on extravagant living, and he found it difficult to write and sell new stories. More trouble came. The hospital where Zelda was confined caught fire and she died in the flames.

Fitzgerald drifted to Hollywood. Here he managed to earn enough from writing magazine stories and motion-picture scripts to put his daughter through college. In 1940 his heart failed while he was working on a novel called *The Last Tycoon*, the story of a movie director, which critics say might have been his masterpiece.

Fitzgerald Is "Rediscovered"

The name Fitzgerald was seldom mentioned by critics for several years following his death, and but few people read his books. Some of his novels were out of print, and his publisher didn't find enough demand to reissue them. Then in 1945, a biography of Fitzgerald, *The Far Side of Paradise* by Arthur Mizener, was published and interest was revived in the spokesman for the "Roaring Twenties." This "redis-covery" of Fitzgerald gained impetus in 1958 with publica-tion of the autobiography of Sheila Graham, Hollywood movie columnist and an intimate friend of Fitzgerald's, which told of his last days. Subsequently, dramatizations of Fitzgerald's life have appeared in the Broadway theater and on American television. Critics have taken a new look at his work and pronounced him one of America's most gifted 20th-century novelists. Readers also have shown new interest in his novels, and most of his books which were out of print have been reissued.

Immensely Readable

Critics and readers agree that Fitzgerald is immensely readable. His style fairly glides along like an accomplished dancer. Here is a sample from his masterpiece, *The Great Gatsby*, the story of a man who grew rich during America's Prohibition days by selling bootleg whisky. "The lights grow brighter as earth lurches away from sun," Fitzgerald wrote, describing a gay New York party. "And now the orchestra is playing yellow cocktail music, and the opera of voices pitches a key higher. Laughter is easier minute by minute, spilled with prodigality, tipped out at a cheerful word. The groups change more swiftly, swell with new arrivals, dissolve and form in the same breath; already there are wanderers, confident girls who weave here and there among the stouter and more stable, become for a sharp, joyous moment the center of a group, and then, excited with triumph, glide on through the sea-change of faces and voices and color under the constantly changing light."

One of America's most distinguished literary critics, John

Peale Bishop, describes Scott Fitzgerald's talents in this way: "Fitzgerald," he said, "was fascinated by the expansive charm and sensational display of the postwar decade in America but . . . when the bills came in he had no coin for their payment. No other writer got under the skin of that particular generation as well as he because he was part of it and its most articulate spokesman. His work has every fault except failure to live."

—Bibliography—

PRINCIPAL WORKS: *This Side of Paradise*, 1920; *Flappers and Philosophers* (short stories), 1920; *The Beautiful and Damned*, 1922; *The Great Gatsby*, 1925; *Tender Is the Night*, 1934; *The Crack-Up* (essays), 1936; *The Last Tycoon*, 1941.

WILLIAM FAULKNER   (1897–1962)

"Man Will Endure Because He Has a Soul"

WILLIAM FAULKNER, Nobel prize winner whose dark, symbol-filled novels provoked a tumult of both admiration and criticism, was himself as much of an enigma as his literary works. Despite his unceasing dedication to his art, he always claimed—and his way of living confirmed his words—that he was not a literary man, but a farmer.

In a rare interview (he scorned reporters and publicity) a few months before his death on July 6, 1962, Faulkner said: "If I had not existed, someone else would have written me, Hemingway, Dostoevsky, all of us. Proof of that is that there are about three candidates for the authorship of Shakespeare's plays. But what is important is *Hamlet* and *Midsummer Night's Dream* and not who wrote them, but that somebody did. The artist is of no importance. Only what he creates is important, since there is nothing new to be said."

Asked whether he felt the writer is under any obligation to the reader, Faulkner replied: "His obligation is to get the work done the best he can do it; whatever obligation he has left over after that he can spend any way he likes. I myself am too busy to care about the public. I have no time to wonder who is reading me. I don't care about John Doe's opinion on my or anyone else's work."

Common Citizen

Indifferent to literary glory, Faulkner felt at home among the earthy, unpretentious people in America's South about whom he wrote—the farmers, the Negro workers, the hunters and fishermen, and the idlers of his small Mississippi home town of Oxford. Short in stature, wiry, with a mustache, Faulkner had the appearance of an aristocratic Mississippi river-boat captain. To outsiders, he seemed silent and unsociable, and he had signs posted up on his farm warning away the curious. But among the farmers and townsmen he was witty and talkative, and loved to drink and swap tall stories with friends in the vacant lot across from the town drugstore.

It was from these common citizens of the southern soil that he created an intricate and obscure world—the rich, dark world of his mythical Yoknapatawpha County; a world full of opaque symbols, odd characters, and complex episodes.

Born in the Deep South near Oxford, Mississippi, the son of a livery-stable owner, Faulkner took little interest in school work; in fact, he never graduated from high school. Later he attended the University of Mississippi, but again found formal study boring and, quitting his classes, drifted to New Orleans. Here he became a friend of Sherwood Anderson, already a famous writer, who saw in him the makings of a great author. It was in New Orleans that Faulkner's first work was published—a poem in a small literary magazine. Both he and his poem, however, attracted little notice. With Anderson's encouragement and help, he published two novels and a book of poems—all unsuccessful.

Writer and Farmer

Unable to live by his pen, he returned to his home town of Oxford where he held several jobs, earning just enough to keep him living and writing. He worked as a house painter and once held a job in the post office, where he was dismissed for lack of attention to duties. For a time he was superintendent of a power plant, spending the late hours of the night writing on an upturned wheelbarrow. It was here that he revised the manuscript of his novel *The Sound and the Fury*, a work which, with its strange stream-of-consciousness style, at first found no publisher. In 1929, when finally the book was issued, critics praised it highly and Faulkner at last was able to earn a living largely by his writing. During the next decade, a stream of novels followed—imaginative and intricate, sometimes bitter and often brilliant.

Questioned about his technique, Faulkner later said: "Let the writer take up surgery or bricklaying if he is interested in technique. There is no mechanical way to get the writing done, no short cut. The young writer would be a fool to follow a theory. Teach yourself by your own mistakes; people learn only by error. The good artist believes nobody is good enough to give him advice. He has supreme vanity.

No matter how much he admires the old writer, he wants to beat him."

Faulkner added, however, that he would not deny the validity of technique. "Sometimes technique," he said, "charges in and takes command of the dream before the writer himself can get his hands on it. That is *tour de force* and the finished work is simply a matter of fitting bricks neatly together."

Faulkner also took his farming seriously. In 1929 he had married a widow with two children. Living in the same century-old house his family had lived in since his childhood, he spent his mornings writing. His afternoons were given to outdoor work, or to hunting and fishing with friends. Then, late in the afternoon, he usually went to visit his mother for tea. His evenings were often spent visiting with old friends and telling jokes and stories.

A Mythical Kingdom

For a long time Faulkner's novels and short stories were appreciated by only a select few, and it was not until a popular edition of his work was published in 1945 that his fame began to widen. The introduction said: "Faulkner performed a labor of imagination that has not been equalled in our time, and a double labor: first, to invent a Mississippi county that was like a mythical kingdom, but was complete and living in all its details; second, to make his story of that county stand as a parable or legend of all the Deep South."

Another writer, Robert Penn Warren, said of Faulkner in 1946: "In mass of work, scope of material, range of effect, reportorial accuracy and symbolic subtlety, in philosophic weight, he can be put beside the masters of our own past literature."

Perhaps the best summing up of Faulkner as an artist and an individual can be taken from his acceptance speech made in Stockholm, Sweden, in 1950 when he was awarded the Nobel prize for literature. He said:

"I feel that this award was not made to me as a man, but to my work—the life's work in the agony and sweat of the human spirit, not for glory and least of all for profit, but to create out of materials of the human spirit something which did not exist there before.

"Man will endure," Faulkner continued, "because he has a soul, a spirit capable of compassion and sacrifice and endurance. The poet's, the writer's duty is to write about these things. It is his privilege to help man endure by lifting his heart, by reminding him of the courage and honor and hope and pride and compassion and pity and sacrifice which have been the glory of his past."

—Bibliography—

PRINCIPAL WORKS: *Soldier's Pay*, 1926; *Sartoris*, 1929; *The Sound and the Fury*, 1929; *As I Lay Dying*, 1930; *Light in August*, 1932; *Absalom, Absalom!*, 1936; *Go Down, Moses, and other Stories*, 1942; *Intruder in the Dust*, 1948; *A Fable*, 1954; *Reivers*, 1962.

ERNEST HEMINGWAY   (1899–1961)

A Life of Adventure

WHAT MAKES a person decide to become an author? Some say it is the urge for self-expression. Others say it is an attempt to escape from the harsh realities of life. Perhaps there is no single explanation.

For the writer, Ernest Hemingway, the famed American, escape—escape from an unhappy love affair—appears to have been the motivating factor which drove him to authorship. Hemingway met the girl, an English nurse, in Italy while recuperating in a hospital from wounds received during World War I. He wanted to marry her and bring her to America. She refused, marrying instead an Italian major. Hemingway was deeply hurt.

Life in Paris

Years passed but he couldn't get the girl off his mind.

Meanwhile, restless and discontented, he moved to Paris and tried to make a living writing, but nobody wanted his manuscripts. One day he was sitting at a sidewalk cafe on the Left Bank complaining to a friend about his ill luck.

"Perhaps the reason you can't sell your work is because you haven't suffered enough; you don't know misery," Hemingway's friend said.

"So I've not known misery!" Hemingway snapped back. "So that's what you think!" Then, at first seemingly lost in memory, he recited the story of his lost love, Agnes, the English nurse. He told his friend about the suffering he had endured in World War I. Later he put the story on paper in the form of a novel, *A Farewell to Arms*. The book was widely read and Hemingway became famous.

Adventure

Hemingway's sixty-two years were packed with excitement. Living through adventure after adventure, he told stories of his life and love on the Left Bank in Paris, of death and bullfights he saw in Spain, fierce game he stalked in the jungles of Africa, wars he fought over Europe, and giant 1,000-pound fish he battled off the coast of Cuba. But his writing was more than just adventure stories; Hemingway helped to set the style for the modern novel. His lean, muscular prose and dramatic plots have, perhaps, been copied more than any other modern author's, and his work has been translated into all the world's major languages.

From boyhood, young Hemingway preferred adventure to a peaceful life. Born in Oak Park, Illinois, on July 21, 1899, the son of a doctor, he spent much of his early days romping through the woods, rifle on his shoulder, or rowing out across the water of a large lake in quest of big fish. Although his family owned a cottage on a lake, he usually slept outside in a tent, the dim light of a kerosene lantern flickering long hours into the night over his makeshift cot as he lay reading.

Cub Reporter

In June, 1917, he graduated from Oak Park High School toward the bottom of his class. Meanwhile war had broken out in Europe and, preferring fighting to college, he tried to enlist in the Army but was rejected because of poor eyesight. Frustrated, he went off to live with an uncle in Kansas City where he found work as a cub reporter on a newspaper. He liked his new writing job, but he still had a compelling urge to get into the war, and the opportunity came not long afterward. While interviewing a group of Italian Red Cross officers early in 1918, young Hemingway learned that Italy was recruiting ambulance drivers to serve on the Italian front. Although only eighteen, he quit his job, signed up, and was soon assigned to Ambulance Unit 4 in Italy.

Brush with Death

Hemingway had been driving behind the lines only a few days when he decided ambulance driving was too safe—in fact, dull. He wanted to be up on the front lines in the thick of things, so he volunteered for canteen service and was soon peddling a bicycle handing out mail, tobacco, and chocolate to soldiers in the trenches. On his tenth day in Italy, as he was handing a chocolate bar to a soldier, a large mortar shell ploughed into the nearby earth. Hemingway was almost buried. His body was filled below the waist with over two hundred and fifty pieces of shrapnel, but after regaining consciousness he rescued a badly wounded Italian soldier and was returning to help others when he was hit again, with a machine-gun bullet, below the left knee.

He spent weeks in a Red Cross hospital, and it was there that he fell in love with his English nurse, Agnes. While in Europe, he received several medals for bravery, then was sent home, limping on a cane. The Hemingway who came back to America was a different person from the youth who had left. War, death, agony, new people, a new language, and love had all been crowded into his life.

Lost Love

While his feet and legs healed, he read a lot and impatiently watched the mail until, one day after receiving a letter, he suddenly became ill. He withdrew from everyone and for days hardly left his room. Finally, with prodding from his family, he revealed that Agnes had written the letter. She wasn't coming to America. She had married an Italian Army major.

Sad and disappointed, Hemingway went to Paris for study and—he hoped—to make a living writing. There he met and became friendly with some of the world's greatest literary figures of that day—James Joyce, Gertrude Stein, Ezra Pound, and others. But despite their advice and help, he couldn't sell his writing. Manuscript after manuscript kept coming back from editors, usually without a single encouraging word—only a printed rejection slip. It was then he met his friend at a sidewalk cafe, took his advice, and drawing on his personal experiences, Hemingway wrote *A Farewell to Arms.*

Success and Travel

Now a successful writer, Hemingway traveled the world, hunting in Africa and the Far East, fishing in numerous oceans and seas. He became fascinated with Spain and bullfighting and lived there for several years. He covered the Spanish Civil War for American newspapers and couldn't resist getting into the fight in Madrid. By then, he was known as "Papa," a bearded hulking bear of a man who joked and swore with the best of the soldiers.

When World War II began, Hemingway, then living in Cuba, armed his own boat as a submarine chaser and restively patrolled the Atlantic coast off the United States. But in 1942 he was in the thick of battle again as a magazine correspondent. He flew from England on bombing missions and became an expert on German rockets. Near the end of the war, he was among the first wave of troops to storm the Normandy beach in 1944.

After the war, he retired to Cuba to fish and write. One book flopped and his critics claimed that "Papa's" career was over.

Nobel Prize

Then in 1952, after years of work, he brought out *The Old Man and the Sea*, a tale of the struggle of a single aging fisherman against the powers of fate and the ocean. It was the story he had been trying to write all his life, and it won him the Pulitzer prize for 1953. The following year he was awarded the Nobel prize for literature.

Suffering from injuries received in plane crashes while hunting wild game in Africa, Hemingway couldn't go to Sweden to receive the Nobel award but in a letter to the academy he declared that the writer's life is a lonely one, and that if he sheds his loneliness his work often deteriorates. A true writer, Hemingway said, should try, with each new book, for something beyond his attainment.

Hemingway, still living in Cuba, continued writing short stories, novels, and magazine articles. But he also began to take life easier, spending more time on his fishing boat with his wife, whom he called "Miss Mary." "No one can work everyday in these hot months without going stale," he wrote during this period. "To break up the pattern of work, we fish the Gulf Stream in the spring and summer months and in the fall."

Last Days

But Hemingway was aging. His hair and beard were already white. His old injuries were bothering him; he had to write standing up and he was sick much of the time. Then Castro took over in Cuba and Hemingway and Miss Mary returned to America, living in Idaho. He spent a few months in hospitals, began losing weight, and saw his creative ability failing. Early one morning in July, 1961, he slipped downstairs in his home, lifted his favorite gun from its rack, and took his own life. Obituary notices darkly spelled out the story on all the front pages of newspapers around the globe.

Perhaps Ernest Hemingway had concluded that like Santiago, the old fisherman in *The Old Man and the Sea,* he had "no luck anymore."

—Bibliography—

PRINCIPAL WORKS: *Three Stories and Ten Poems*, 1923; *The Torrents of Spring*, 1926; *The Sun Also Rises*, 1926; *A Farewell to Arms*, 1929; *Death in the Afternoon*, 1932; *To Have and Have Not*, 1937; *For Whom the Bell Tolls*, 1940; *Across the River and into the Trees*, 1950; *The Old Man and the Sea*, 1952.

ERSKINE CALDWELL   (1903–   )

America's Most Widely Published Novelist

A TALL, ruggedly built, friendly man with hair so red his friends call it pink, Erskine Caldwell, author of *Tobacco Road*, has published more than thirty books since he began writing in the early thirties. Today, with more than fifty million copies in print in nineteen countries, Caldwell's works are among the world's top-selling novels.

Success for him, as for most other writers, did not come easily. Caldwell wrote for at least seven years, he says, before he was able to get a book published. During this period he turned out more than a hundred short stories and several novels, many of which he submitted to publishers only to receive quick rejection slips.

Burned Old Work
After his first story was published, he made a big bonfire

and burned everything he had written before then, considering his earlier work as practice. Nor has writing become much easier for Caldwell with the passing years. Each story he writes today is rewritten from fifteen to twenty times. "Writing," he has said, "is just a combination of trial and error." Once a story is completed, Caldwell rarely will permit a publisher to change a line or even a word of his manuscript. If a paragraph, line, or word makes sense to him, he declares, he feels it will make sense to the reader and he sees no reason to change it. It's not, he says, that he doesn't welcome criticism; it's just that after he has written and rewritten a story many times, he feels he knows more about it than an editor.

Rarely Reads Other Authors

Caldwell also says he rarely reads any other author's books —he's much too busy with his own. Asked once by a reporter whether he had read "any good books by other authors lately," he replied: "Asking a writer whether he has read any good books by other authors lately is like asking a doctor if he's taken any good medicine lately."

Caldwell's most famous works tell of the hardships of tenant farmers in America's South during the depression years of the thirties—the period when Caldwell first emerged as a talented young writer. One such book, *God's Little Acre*, published in 1934, has sold over nine million copies, an all-time record for a novel in the United States. The main character in *God's Little Acre* is Ty Ty, a poor Georgia farmer who spends much of his time futilely digging for gold in his yard when he might have made at least a fair living had he devoted the same labor to tilling his acres.

Caldwell's second best-known work, *Tobacco Road*, also has its setting in his native Georgia and is centered about the life of a poor cotton farmer, Lester Jeeter, who loses his farm through lack of initiative and enterprise. In Shakespeare's time, both books would have been called comedies of error. Although grim tales, they are brightened throughout with flashes of broad humor.

Born in Rural Georgia

Caldwell was born in rural Georgia, so far from a railroad or post office his birthplace is said to have had no name. His father, a Protestant minister who served as secretary of his church, was required by his duties to move frequently, and until he reached the age of twenty young Caldwell rarely stayed in any one place longer than six months. His home, he says, was the entire South from Virginia to Florida, from the Atlantic Ocean to the Pacific—a constant change of faces and surroundings.

With his family moving around so often, Caldwell seldom had a chance to attend a single school very long. He went to a primary school in Virginia for one year, attended grammar school in Tennessee for one year and high school in Georgia for about one year. His mother taught him the rest of the time.

Odd Job Worker

When Caldwell was eighteen, he enrolled in a small college in South Carolina, but restlessness soon overcame him and he went to sea on a boat running guns for revolutionaries in Central America. He left the ship there, stayed in Central America for a time, then decided to continue his education at the University of Virginia. Working nights in a poolroom to pay for his room and board, Caldwell studied at Virginia for a year. But again becoming restless, he went to Pennsylvania, where he worked in a variety store, played professional football, managed a lecture tour for a British soldier of fortune, and sold building lots.

After this period of odd jobs, he returned to the University of Virginia, but soon realized formal education was not for him. He next found work as a newspaper reporter on the *Atlanta Journal*, hoping to improve his writing skill so that he could make his living as a short-story writer. Soon tiring of newspaper reporting and unable to write salable stories, he moved to Maine determined to stay until he wrote a story which satisfied him. After five years of writing— meanwhile making his living by cutting wood and growing potatoes—he wrote a story in 1933 which received a $1,000 prize from the *Yale Review*, literary publication of Yale University. The following year *God's Little Acre* was published, bringing its author fame and fortune.

As befits a widely read author, Erskine Caldwell lives today in a big house perched atop a high hill in a fashionable district of San Francisco with a magnificent view of the bay. In fact, the view is so fine, Caldwell feels it necessary to pull down the shades to get in a mood for his nine-to-five work-day. In the evening he and his wife often dine out at one of the famous San Francisco restaurants.

—Bibliography—

PRINCIPAL WORKS: *Tobacco Road*, 1932; *God's Little Acre*, 1934; *Kneel to the Rising Sun* (short stories), 1935; *You Have Seen*

Their Faces (with Margaret Bourke-White, non-fiction), 1937; *Georgia Boy*, 1943; *Complete Stories of Erskine Caldwell*, 1953; *Love and Money*, 1954; *Claudelle Inglish*, 1958; *Around About America*, 1964.

LANGSTON HUGHES　　　(1902–1967)

Dedicated Negro Poet

ONE AFTERNOON in 1925, a twenty-three-year-old Negro bus boy approached the famous poet and lecturer Vachel Lindsay in the lobby of the Wardman Park Hotel in Washington, D.C., and timorously asked the noted author if he would care to have a look at some of his poetry.

The young Negro, who often went hungry in childhood, had been writing stories and poems since elementary school. They dealt mostly with his hard life, and he wrote them in the hope of bettering the living conditions of his race.

Lindsay, always sympathetic to young writers, liked the poems and read three of them that night to his lecture audience. The event was of great importance to Langston Hughes. It introduced him to the American public, and in the years that followed he came to be known as the poet laureate of the Negro people.

Spokesman for His People

Today Hughes is recognized as one of the world's out-standing Negro authors of the 20th century, attaining that position not only because of the high quality of his writing but also because he was a dedicated spokesman for the Negro people. Hughes' works—poems, plays, novels, essays, and several anthologies and histories—often deal with the tribulations of his race, as well as with their consoling joys. Typical of his poems expressing joy and pride in his race are these lines from "My People":

> The night is beautiful,
> So the faces of my people.
> The stars are beautiful,
> So the eyes of my people.
> Beautiful, also, is the sun,
> Beautiful, also, are the souls of my people.

Born February 1, 1902 in Joplin, Missouri, Hughes grew up in nearby Lawrence, Kansas. In his autobiography, *The Big Sea*, he describes a childhood harried by dread of "the mortgage man" and not having enough to eat. But there were some compensations—his grandmother's recollections of the famous abolitionist John Brown, his grandfather's passion for freedom and justice, and his uncle's success as a United States minister to Haiti. These all tended to make Hughes more aware of the problems of the Negro, and he was determined to make others aware, too.

Class Poet

Fired with ambition to secure greater economic and social justice for members of his race, the youth began to write poems and stories, mostly about his own experiences. They were good enough to win him the honor of being named class poet in the eighth grade of high school. A little later when his family moved to Cleveland, Ohio, Hughes joined the staff of the Central High School literary magazine and became editor of the yearbook.

Graduating at seventeen, he traveled the world for the next five years in an attempt to broaden his experience and examine a wider range of Negro life. He took all kinds of jobs. He was a ranch hand in Mexico, a cook in Paris night clubs, and a seaman on a freighter running to Europe and Africa. Meanwhile he never stopped writing poetry. He wrote about Harlem, the section of New York City peopled mainly by Negroes; of Africa, the birthplace of his race; and about individuals whose problems and aspirations appealed to him.

"The Weary Blues"

After Vachel Lindsay read Hughes' poetry in public in 1925 and the Negro poet began to attract a following, he was awarded first prize in a literary contest conducted by *Opportunity*, a journal of Negro life. The award also resulted in the publication of his first volume of poems, issued under the title *The Weary Blues*.

Other successes followed. Hughes received a scholarship to Lincoln University in Pennsylvania, where he was graduated in 1929. He now found himself in demand as a lecturer, traveling widely throughout the South, where he spoke at Negro high schools and universities. Everywhere he went, he encouraged Negro writers and poets, believing that if living and working conditions among members of his race were to improve, there must be more Negro spokesmen for his people. In 1934 the late Dr. Charles A. Beard, famed historian, praised Hughes for his "socially conscious" attitude, naming him as one of America's most interesting people. When civil war broke out in Spain, Hughes became the only Negro newspaper correspondent to cover the conflict. Returning to the United States, he found an outlet for his love of the drama, becoming executive director of the Harlem Suitcase Theatre, the only Negro repertory theater in New York City.

"Simple"

During World War II, Hughes wrote radio scripts and other wartime morale-building programs and gave poetry recitals in soldier recreation centers from coast to coast. In 1945 he became a columnist for the *Chicago Defender*, where his short stories about a fictitious Negro character called "Simple" first appeared. Simple, a genial, fun-loving, talkative Harlem Negro, is probably the most beloved of all characters in contemporary Negro literature and has found his way into books, radio, television, and even the musical-comedy stage.

Hughes also co-authored and edited several Negro histories and anthologies. In 1949 he co-edited *The Poetry of the Negro*, considered by critics the most significant anthology in its field. His *Pictorial History of the Negro in America*, published in 1956, gave for the first time an authoritative, panoramic picture-story of almost every aspect of Negro life—social, political, artistic, and economic. And his *Fight for Freedom: The Story of the National Association for the Advancement of Colored People*, written in 1962, is recognized as an excellent contribution to the history of the Negro in North America.

Work Widely Translated

Hughes received numerous fellowships, taught creative writing in Atlanta and Chicago universities, and lectured extensively in America, Europe, and the West Indies. Unlike many other Negro writers who became expatriates, Hughes settled in New York where he lived until his death.

Hughes' poems, stories, articles, and other writing are often brilliant in technique. His works are widely read and have been translated into several languages, including Chinese. Some of his poems have been set to music. He brought to his work a sharp ear for folk speech and song, and made frequent use of jazz rhythm and colloquial expression. Many, though by no means all, of his poems are in Negro dialect, as is this excerpt from *The Weary Blues:*

> In deep song voice with a melancholy tone
> I heard that Negro sing, that old piano moan—
> Ain't got nobody in all this world,
> Ain't got nobody but ma self.
> I's gwine to quit ma frownin'
> And put ma troubles on the shelf.

Much of Hughes' writing, like his life, was dedicated to improving the condition of American Negroes, and he saw great progress among the race in his lifetime. And yet he lived to see his gentle approach to Negro problems rejected and ridiculed by strident voices, noisy marches, and violence. To angry young Negroes who sought quick answers to old, complex, and often prejudice-ridden questions,

Langston Hughes was old fashioned and outmoded, a relic of less turbulent times.

And although the final verdict rests in the future, Hughes, with his messages couched in gentle irony and compassionate humor, may well have the last laugh. Long after the angry marches have ceased and the noisy, shouting demonstrations are forgotten, his poems and stories will probably be remembered as a powerful force in awakening America's conscience to the plight of the Negro. "Humor," he once said, "is a weapon, too, of no mean value against one's foes."

And because he believed that only through democratic processes can the Negro become a fully accepted member of society, his writing often combines the realistic admission of temporary or past defeat for his race with an optimistic conviction that the United States will soon fulfill the Negro's hopes and dreams. As he says in the concluding lines of his poem, "Let America Be America Again":

> O, yes,
> I say it plain,
> America never was America to me,
> And yet I swear this oath—
> America will be.

—Bibliography—

PRINCIPAL WORKS: Poetry—*The Weary Blues*, 1926; *Dear Lovely Death*, 1931; *Shakespeare in Harlem*, 1942; *Freedom's Plow*, 1943; *Selected Poems*, 1959. Prose—*Simple Speaks His Mind*, 1950; *Simple Takes a Wife*, 1953; *Simple's Uncle Sam*, 1965. General—*Langston Hughes Reader*, 1958.

PEARL BUCK (1892–   )

Asia Is Her Bailiwick

WESTERNERS for centuries have tried to describe the life and customs of Oriental peoples, but few have been as successful in bridging the gap in cultures between East and West as Pearl Buck, American novelist and 1938 Nobel prize winner for literature. Many consider Mrs. Buck's short stories, biographies, and novels required reading for Westerners seeking to understand the Asian mind.

Lived in China

Pearl Buck spent much of her early life in China, and it was through her experience there, she says, that she became "mentally bifocal"—blessed with the ability to look clearly at two cultures, East and West, at once and to love them both. Born Pearl Sydenstricker in a small West Virginia town in 1892, she was taken to China by her missionary parents when she was only five months old. Her childhood, spent in Chinkiang on the banks of the Yangtse River, provided a background for much of her writing and her appreciation of Oriental life.

Reared in the Chinese community itself, not in the area set aside for foreigners, Pearl learned to speak Chinese even before she could speak English. Her playmates were mostly Chinese and she often visited their homes, learning Oriental customs and traditions passed down for many generations. Looking back on those childhood years, she recalls that "I had almost ceased to think of myself as different, if indeed I ever thought so, from the Chinese."

Boxer Rebellion

Then in 1900, eight-year-old Pearl suddenly became acutely aware that she was a foreigner. Her family was forced to flee for safety during the Boxer Rebellion. This incident may well have caused her to discover the misunderstanding that sometimes exists between the Eastern and Western cultures of which she is a part—a misunderstanding most of her later literary career has been spent trying to correct.

With the rebellion over, Pearl and her family returned to Chinkiang. At the age of seventeen she came to the United States for the first time since her infancy, entering Randolph-Macon Women's College in Virginia. She had decided to become a writer and in her senior year won two school literary prizes. After graduating, she taught for one semester, but upon receiving news that her mother was ill she returned to China.

Marries Missionary

In 1917, after her mother's recovery and several years of teaching in a Chinese elementary school, she married Dr. John Buck, an American missionary who specialized in teaching agriculture. They spent their first five years of marriage in North China, but when her husband was transferred to Nanking University, they moved to that city, where Pearl Buck began teaching English. One afternoon in August, 1922, she sat down at her typewriter and wrote a short essay which she called "In China, Too." The piece was accepted by *The Atlantic Monthly*, one of America's best-known magazines, and the literary career of Pearl Buck was thereby launched.

While continuing to teach, she began her first novel, *East Wind: West Wind*. This work, although not a notable success, gave the young novelist the confidence she needed to devote herself full-time to her next and probably greatest book, *The Good Earth*, which won her the Pulitzer prize and immediate world-wide literary acclaim.

Miss Buck's handling of *The Good Earth*—combining her Chinese roots, her American heritage, and an overriding desire to explain Oriental culture to the West—was highly praised by critics. The book has been translated into Japanese and more than thirty other languages, and is considered by many critics the most distinguished work of American fiction published between 1930 and 1935. *The Good Earth*, however, was more than just a successful book. It made its author the foremost interpreter of Asiatic civilization to the Western world and became itself a literary bridge between Asia and America.

Wins Nobel Prize

For the remainder of the 1930's, during which Mrs. Buck moved to the United States, she continued writing novels, most meeting more modest success than *The Good Earth*. But they did bring about greater understanding and appreciation of the Orient. Her fame grew, and in 1938 she became the first American woman to win the Nobel prize for literature. The Nobel prize committee called her novels "outstanding in their rich and genuine epic portrayals of Chinese peasant life."

Meanwhile, Mrs. Buck was devoting her life to the same aims as her works. In 1941 she founded The East and West Association, an organization described as "an educational experiment designed for friendship and mutual understanding between peoples, especially of Asia and the United States." The Association brought lecturers and entertainers from Asia to America and sponsored their tours to communities all over the country to speak and demonstrate their way of life. With her second husband, Richard J. Walsh, she published *Asia Magazine*, dedicated to forging further ties between the two cultures.

After World War II, Mrs. Buck's writing became more diversified. She wrote novels about Japan, many children's books, novels set in America, and two volumes of autobiography. But her interest in promoting Asian-American friendship did not change. In 1949 she founded Welcome House, a nonprofit organization for the care and adoption of American-born children of Asiatic ancestry. Near her Green Hills Farm home in Pennsylvania are two houses where the children—Chinese, Korean, Japanese, and others —live until suitable foster parents can be found for them.

"The Living Reed"

Pearl Buck's work has long been popular in Korea and her novel *The Living Reed,* written in much the same manner as she wrote about China in *The Good Earth,* aims at portraying the spirit of Korea. The book traces three generations of the family of Kim Il-han, adviser to the imperial throne in 1881, who labor for the salvation of their homeland. Interwoven with three love themes, the trials and suffering of the Kim clan often rise to the level of poetic allegory, for Pearl Buck sees the Kims not merely as a family but as a symbol of a proud nation.

Today, Mrs. Buck, described as a tall, "severely handsome" woman with gray hair, is still active, both as a writer and as the mother of six children. Her literary works now number over forty. Although she considers herself a writer in the Chinese tradition of fiction which stresses entertainment as its primary purpose, she is especially proud of the role her novels play in serving as a window through which two civilizations can gaze upon each other and learn from each other.

—Bibliography—

PRINCIPAL WORKS: *East Wind: West Wind,* 1929; *The Good Earth,* 1931; *The Mother,* 1934; *Dragon Seed,* 1942; *Stories of China, Japan and America,* 1947; *The Hidden Flower,* 1952; *The Living Reed,* 1963.

THORNTON WILDER (1897–)

Dramatist of Time and Space

IT HAS BEEN said that when astronauts finally land on the moon, they should not be surprised if they were greeted by Thornton Wilder, an American author who has made the universe his dramatic home. By experience, talent, and temperamental necessity, Wilder has created a literary world beyond time and space—a world through which he seems to move as easily as a child through his home-town streets.

"The Skin of Our Teeth"

Wilder's brilliant success in cheating time and space is accomplished not only by the mingling of the serious and comic but also by such devices as letting his actors step out of their roles to discuss with the audience their own views on the play, or to air their personal problems. Wilder's ability to telescope time and to give added dimensions to his work perhaps is most fully developed in *The Skin of Our Teeth*, in which the story of a single American family recapitulates the entire history of the human race.

The Skin of Our Teeth was first produced in 1942, but the play is timeless, dramatically presenting the dilemmas and frustrations which mankind faces with the recurrence of such discouraging totalitarian systems as fascism, Nazism, and communism.

Yet despite the grim and seemingly unending problems which bedevil the characters down through the centuries, *The Skin of Our Teeth* is far from a saga of despair. Wilder's theme is that despite nature's destructive powers and man's continuing follies—ignorance, cruelty, indifference, and cowardice—the human race somehow manages to survive and inch ahead.

Wilder's Life

Thornton Wilder was born on April 17, 1897, in Madison, Wisconsin, where his father was the editor of a newspaper. When Thornton was nine years old, his father became U.S. Consul General in China, and the boy spent a year and a half there in missionary schools. He prepared for Oberlin College at high schools in California. Finishing his sophomore year at Oberlin, he went to Yale, dropping out for a year in 1918 to serve in the Coast Artillery Corps before receiving his A.B. degree in 1920. He spent another year studying archeology at the American Academy in Rome. During the following seven years (1921–28) he taught French and was a housemaster at Lawrenceville School in New Jersey, except for a two-year leave of absence for study and writing. Meanwhile he had begun taking graduate work at Princeton, where he was awarded his M.A. degree in 1926.

Wilder continued his writing and teaching until 1942 when he joined the U.S. Air Force, serving in Africa and Italy until 1945. He now lives in Hamden, Connecticut, but travels widely, spending much of his time abroad. He has taught at both the University of Chicago and Harvard, and has held seminars and given lectures at many foreign universities. Wilder still thinks of himself first of all as an educator.

Teacher and Writer

Although Wilder began his career as a teacher of literature and a writer of short novels, it is in the field of the experimental theater that he has achieved his greatest success. Without issuing manifestoes, he quietly turned the theater inside out and upside down for his purposes. His two most famous plays—*Our Town* (1938) and *The Skin of Our Teeth*—achieve the rare distinction of being experimental without being frantic. In *Our Town*, for example, for most of two acts, the playwright invites members of his audience to examine Grover's Corners, a small American community, as though they were seeing it—in his own words —"at ever greater distances through a telescope." The characters and events are taken not so much from life as from the bittersweet folklore of life in any small town. Then suddenly the telescope zooms in for a close-up.

Our Town has been called a hymn to everyday living. Emily, one of the principal characters, has just died, and is given a chance to relive one day in her life. She chooses her twelfth birthday. On earth again, she revels in the occasion with all the intensity of first awareness. And then the time comes to leave. Every one of her senses—and ours—is engaged. "Good-by, Good-by world," Emily says. "Good-by Grover's Corners . . . Mama and Papa. Good-by to clocks ticking . . . and Mama's sunflowers. And food and coffee. And new ironed dresses and hot baths . . . and sleeping and waking up. Oh, earth you're too wonderful for anybody to realize you."

Out of this moment of engagement comes Emily's immortal cry: "Do any human beings ever realize life while they live it?—every, every minute?"

Wilder does not stop there. The telescope pulls back to the stars—"doing their old crisscross journeys in the sky"— pausing only long enough for a dispassionate glance at Emily's mourning husband. It is a compassionate moment that lingers in the memory. *Our Town* is universal in its appeal, and if Wilder had written nothing else this play alone would have placed him well in the forefront of American authors.

"The Bridge of San Luis Rey"

Thornton Wilder is best known as a dramatist, but he has also written novels of distinction, his most famous being *The Bridge of San Luis Rey* (1927) which was greeted on publication with such laudatory comments as "a little masterpiece," "sensitive and beautiful," and "a novel instinct with pure grace." It is the story of five persons who were hurled to their death on July 20, 1714, when the bridge they were crossing on a Peruvian highway collapsed.

Why were these particular five people thrown to their death by the accident—if an accident it was? Was it blind chance, was it the hand of God, or were these five in some way the authors of their own death? Wilder doesn't attempt to answer the questions asked. He does, however, offer an answer to one question which might have been asked: Is lavished love, although frustrated, wasted?

The abbess at the Convent of Santa Maria, whose life is consecrated to the work of the Lord, reflects upon this question at the close of the book. "Soon," she says, "we shall die and all memory of these five will have left the earth." Nevertheless, she adds, the love they gave "will have been enough. . . . There is a land of the living and a land of the dead and the bridge is love, the only survival, the only meaning."

Fascinated by the Theater

Although Wilder is not a prolific writer, published work includes six novels, six full-length plays, numerous short plays, and several translated dramas, as well as an opera libretto and a variety of articles, reviews, and lectures. He has also done some writing in foreign tongues.

Today the barrel-chested, gray-haired Wilder is an anomaly of gentleness and scholarliness in the rough-and-tumble theater world. He preserves an engaging attitude, an apprenticeship toward his craft. He has always been fascinated by the specific techniques of the theater and its nature as a collective enterprise. "Many plays—certainly mine," he once said, "are like blank checks. The actors and directors put their signatures upon them."

In recent years Wilder has been working on a cycle of experimental plays. His desire for the new, the untried in dramatic expression seems as strong as ever. He prefers the arena stage, and for good reason: his plays are eminently suited for it. "All over the world," Wilder says, "the theater is flowing back to a freer stage, one projecting out into the audience and giving more intimacy."

Thornton Wilder loves the theater, believes America is "the most theater-infatuated nation in all history," and prefers comedy in private life as well as on stage: "I erase as I go along," he says. "I look forward so much I have only an imperfect memory of the past."

—Bibliography—

PRINCIPAL WORKS: Fiction—*The Cabala*, 1925; *The Bridge of San Luis Rey*, 1927; *The Woman of Andros*, 1930; *Heaven's My Destination*, 1935. Plays—*Our Town*, 1938; *The Skin of Our Teeth*, 1942; *The Matchmaker*, 1955.

TENNESSEE WILLIAMS   (1914–   )

The "Black Play"

TENNESSEE WILLIAMS has been both praised as America's greatest living playwright and criticized as thriving on melodrama. Few, however, will deny the power of his plays nor the vitality of the wide assortment of characters—most of them dark, brooding, and unhappy—who people his dramas: truck drivers, prostitutes, poets, housewives, politicians, and priests.

Williams admits that his plays contain a large measure of violence, neuroticism, and sex, but he explains that if he is to write at all, he must write about characters and situations which correspond to his own inner tensions. "Frankly there must be some limitations to me as a dramatist," he once said in an interview. "I can't handle people in routine situations. . . . If these people are excessively melodramatic, well, it should be remembered that a play must concentrate

142

the events of a lifetime in the short span of a three-act play. Of necessity, these events must be more violent than life."

Self-Pity Is His Theme

Even though Tennessee Williams confesses his deep involvement in emotionalism, critics have pointed out that his plays deal consistently with a serious theme—self-pity, the persistence of memory that holds people in its grip and will not let them go on with their lives.

In fact, Williams' first successful play, *The Glass Menagerie,* produced in 1943, is a story told from memory by Tom Wingfield, an aspiring poet, who is both narrator and one of the chief characters in the drama. The title is symbolic: Laura, a shy, withdrawn girl crippled by a childhood illness, has a collection of miniature glass animals in which she takes refuge from the realities of life. Amanda, mother of Tom and Laura, embittered by the memory of a husband who deserted her, compounds the problems of her children by persisting in living in a past which can never be recaptured. The play ends with Tom wandering aimlessly about the world, plagued by bitter memories of his unhappy childhood and youth, and with Laura still living in the make-believe world of her glass menagerie.

The Glass Menagerie made Tennessee Williams world famous, and as the years passed, his stature rose rapidly with the production of other widely known dramas, notably *A Streetcar Named Desire, Cat on a Hot Tin Roof,* and, more recently, *Night of the Iguana.*

Born in Mississippi

Born in Columbus, Mississippi, on March 26, 1914,

Williams spent his early years in the warm protection of an Episcopal rectory where his grandfather was clergyman. During this period, Williams' life was serene and uncomplicated. But when he was twelve, his father, a traveling salesman, moved his family to St. Louis, Missouri, where he had accepted an office position with a shoe manufacturing company. Leaving the rectory was a great tragedy for the boy, who found difficulty adjusting to new social surroundings.

The "ugly row of apartment buildings," as Williams called them, where he lived in St. Louis, was not far from an exclusive area where the wealthy lived in fine residences set on beautiful lawns. The affluent life of the rich aroused shock and envy in Williams, setting off a rebellion that greatly influenced his work. It was the beginning of the social consciousness which has marked most of his writing.

After completing his high school education in St. Louis, Williams entered a St. Louis college but dropped out after two years for lack of money to take a clerical job in the shoe company where his father worked. Meanwhile, he had begun to write short stories in his spare time. He was unable to sell any of his early writing, however, and his disappointment over his failure was said to have contributed to a breakdown in his health. Quitting his job in the shoe company in 1936, he went to Memphis, Tennessee, to live with his grandfather, who had retired from the ministry. From this period, Williams began to succeed with his writing and was able to return to college, graduating from the University of Iowa in 1938. The next two years, he traveled about the United States working at odd jobs—running an elevator, reciting verse in Greenwich Village, operating a teletype, working in a restaurant, and ushering in the Strand Theater on Broadway.

Wrote in Hollywood

While working as an usher his writing attracted the attention of a major motion-picture studio, which hired him at a salary of $250 a week. He spent six months in Hollywood, saving enough money to support himself while he wrote *The Glass Menagerie*. The play was first produced in Chicago where initially it attracted little attention. The producers, however, had great faith in the then-unknown Tennessee Williams' potential as a playwright. Believing *The Glass Menagerie* would be successful on Broadway and have a better chance there of winning the famed Pulitzer prize, they moved it to New York. The play failed to win the coveted prize, but it did win the New York Drama Critics' Circle Award for 1944. From this point on, fame and success were his.

Poems and Short Stories

Not all of Williams' talents have been directed toward writing plays. In 1956, he published a volume of poetry, *In the Winter of Cities*, which some critics claim would have entitled him to fame had he not written a line for the stage. The poems explain much about Williams' inner feelings and thoughts.

Typical of Williams' poetry is an eight-line piece called "Cortege" which could easily be an outline for one of his bitterly pessimistic one-act plays:

> Cold, cold, cold
> was the merciless blood of your father
>
> By the halo of his breath
> your mother knew him . . .

Loathing the touch
of the doorknob he had clasped

Hating the napkin
he had used at the table.

Like the plays, his poems are based on his wanderings,
his observations, and his conviction that human love is
forever battering itself to pieces on the reefs of ignorance
and misunderstanding.

May Be Mellowing

As Williams entered his fifties, there were indications that
he was mellowing. "I'm through with what have been
called my 'black plays,'" he said after the production in
1960 of his *Period of Adjustment*. "I'll still deal with life and
reality of course—and sometimes caustically, perhaps, but
I won't be pointing out the bestiality in life.

"Bestiality still exists, but I don't want to write about it
anymore. I want to pass the rest of my life believing in
other things. I was too preoccupied with the destructive
impulses. From now on I want to be concerned with the
kinder aspects of life. Maybe these non-black plays won't
be all white, but I hope to cast a kinder shadow, with more
concentration on the quieter elements of existence."

—Bibliography—

PRINCIPAL WORKS: Plays—*The Glass Menagerie*, 1945; *A
Streetcar Named Desire*, 1947; *The Rose Tattoo*, 1951; *Camino Real*,
1953; *Cat on a Hot Tin Roof*, 1955; *Orpheus Descending* 1957;
Night of the Iguana, 1961. Poetry—*In the Winter of Cities*, 1956.

ARTHUR MILLER (1915–)

Spokesman of the "Little Man"

ARTHUR MILLER, whose play *Death of a Salesman* is known to audiences around the world, confesses that he had no taste for literature when he was growing up, and that until the age of seventeen he never read a book weightier than two popular American juveniles, *Tom Swift* and *The Rover Boys*. That this seemingly untalented youth, who failed several subjects in high school and had no taste for literature, was to earn a fortune as a famous dramatist numbered among America's intellectuals is one of the 20th century's biggest success stories.

Miller first attracted the attention of American theatergoers with the 1947 production of his tightly knit, superbly written *All My Sons*, with its universal theme of man's personal greed versus his concern for his fellowman. The production two years later of *Death of a Salesman* assured

147

Miller's position as one of the nation's foremost dramatists.

Classical drama has been defined as something being done—a compound of action, motion, and emotion. In this sense, Miller cannot be called a classical dramatist, for in all of his works it is ideas, thoughts, feelings, which are of uppermost importance. He is not so much a social critic as an evaluator and sympathizer with the "little man" caught up in passions and dilemmas beyond his understanding. Willy Loman in *Death of a Salesman*—the pathetic, perennial failure, entangled in his own dreams of glory, his continuous self-delusion, and his fanatical faith in his older son—is a typical Miller "anti-hero." He is, perhaps, Miller's greatest character creation.

Football before Literature

Arthur Miller was born in 1915 in New York and grew up in a Brooklyn suburb, a rough-and-tumble neighborhood that later provided the background for his playlet *A View from the Bridge*. A tall, rawboned boy, football was his primary passion in high school, but at the University of Michigan he met and was greatly influenced by Professor Kenneth H. Rowe, an understanding and intelligent teacher of drama. Young Arthur Miller became so fired with enthusiasm and ideas at Michigan that he won the University's annual Avery Hopwood Drama Award for two consecutive years.

He left college in 1938 and joined the Writers Project of the Federal Theater, a government undertaking started during the depression years to assist unemployed writers and artists. This project was discontinued after four months, leaving Miller free to devote his talents to radio script-writing and further attempts at playwrighting. He settled down in Brooklyn with his wife, a former classmate from the University of Michigan, but then came World War II. Miller discovered that an old football injury disqualified him from military service, and, unable to earn a living from his writing, he found work as a steam fitter in the Brooklyn Navy Yard, continuing in his spare time to turn out patriotic scripts and one-act plays.

Worked on Ernie Pyle Script

Toward the end of the war he was assigned to work on the script of the movie *The Story of G. I. Joe*, based on the life of Ernie Pyle, the famed American war correspondent who was killed on Okinawa. Miller spent six months with the U.S. Infantry on maneuvers gathering information for the film. In 1944 he published the material from his research on the movie in a book entitled *Situation Normal*.

A year later Miller published a novel called *Focus*, which dealt with racial conflicts in the United States. Meanwhile he continued to work at playwrighting, and in 1944 his first recognized play, *The Man Who Had All the Luck*, was presented.

The year 1947 saw the production of *All My Sons*, and two years later, the critically acclaimed *Death of a Salesman*. Arthur Miller's place in the American theater was firmly established. Since that time his stature as a dramatist has grown, although personal tragedies such as his unhappy marriage to Marilyn Monroe, the film actress, and his troubles with the Congressional Committee on Un-American Activities have earned him unfavorable publicity as well as some sympathy. His recent drama *After the Fall*, produced in New York City, was highly praised by some critics, but ripped apart by others as an unnecessarily cruel treatment of the foibles and weaknesses of Miss Monroe.

"All My Sons"

Of the Miller plays, *All My Sons* probably comes closest to classical tradition, and is the most easily described and defined. It is a tightly knit story, progressing logically from one event to another, every action and each character acting and interacting in a sequence which brings the play to what the audience feels is an unavoidable conclusion. The plot of *All My Sons* is basically simple. Joe Keller, a highly successful businessman, made much money during the war. But also during that time, his firm was accused of selling defective parts to the Air Force, thus causing the death of a number of young men. Joe has succeeded in placing the blame for this deal on his partner, who was sent to prison. At the close of the play, in the final agonizing scene, Joe tells his family that he did it all for them, he did it for his sons, and his one surviving son reminds him bitterly that all the young men who died because of Joe's deliberate dishonesty were his sons also.

"Death of a Salesman"

Miller demonstrated in *Death of a Salesman*, perhaps his best-known play, his answer to critics of his earlier dramas who claimed he was incapable of producing other than a "conventional" play. In *Death of a Salesman*, Miller proved that he could progress beyond the ordinary concept of time and place writing. He himself declared, "The conventional play form squeezed the humanity out of a play. Why shouldn't a play have the depth, the completeness, and diversity of a novel?"

Most critics agree that *Death of a Salesman* is Miller's finest work. Wolcott Gibbs, writing in *The New Yorker*, called it a "tremendously affecting work . . . told with a mixture of compassion, imagination, and hard technical competence you don't often find in the theater today." It is the story of Willy Loman, a little man with many dreams and delusions. As the play progresses, he loses his job, discovers that his idealized older son is a failure, and that his younger son, though successful in business, is morally rotten. In the end Willy has lost everything, including his own self-respect, and has nothing more to lose except his life. It is Willy's particular tragedy that even in dying he can save none— himself, his wife, nor the sons whom he loves so selfishly and so deeply. In this play, Miller gives us a new dimension in playwrighting—a new form. Memory and interpolation become part of the play's progress. It becomes necessary for the theatergoer to look backward as well as forward as the play proceeds.

Some feel, however, that *The Crucible* is Miller's greatest play. Here the author returns to the religious origins of drama in a truly magnificent play, reflecting, in its theme of hysterical religious persecution, the contemporary ordeal which the author at that time was himself facing—his own investigation by a Congressional Committee. Miller himself says that in writing *The Crucible* he wished to show that the sin of "public terror is that it divests man of conscience, of himself." *The Crucible* is a dramatic retelling of the historic Salem witch trials of 1692–93 in New England during which hundreds were arrested and twenty persons were put to death. The ordeal begins when a group of hysterical young girls accuse first a Negro slave and then a number of prominent citizens, men and women, of witchcraft. During the general hysteria which follows, the judges are caught up in the blind fanaticism of the time and justice fails. The hero, John Proctor, is accused by one of the young girls whose advances he had formerly rejected. Although he is given a chance to save himself by acknowledging his guilt, he chooses instead to stand firmly by his principles and die.

Minor Plays

In his plays Miller demonstrates what he calls the "tragic victory"—the hero or protagonist who takes his own life as in *All My Sons* and *Death of a Salesman,* or chooses deliberately to die at the hands of others, as in *The Crucible* and *A View from the Bridge.*

Miller's two works *A Memory of Two Mondays* and *A View from the Bridge,* although of less importance, have helped to confirm his reputation as one of America's foremost playwrights. *A View from the Bridge,* originally a one-act play, later was expanded into two acts for production on Broadway.

Miller's writing is concise, his staging dramatic, and his characters sharp and finely drawn. Even his minor characters are skillfully conceived and developed, coming across the stage as believable, living people. Much of the strength of Miller's writing, in fact, lies in the authenticity of his characterization. Even if Arthur Miller never writes another play, most critics are confident his *All My Sons, Death of a Salesman,* and *The Crucible,* have established him as one of this century's most important American dramatists.

—Bibliography—

PRINCIPAL WORKS: *The Man Who Had All the Luck*, 1944; *All My Sons*, 1947; *Death of a Salesman*, 1949; *The Crucible*, 1953; *A View from the Bridge*, 1955; *After the Fall*, 1964.

JOHN DOS PASSOS (1896–)

Historian of the American Scene

WHAT IS the relationship between a writer and the generation of which he is a part? John Dos Passos gave his answer to this question in the introduction to *Three Soldiers,* one of his earlier novels. "The mind of a generation," he wrote, "is its speech. A writer makes aspects of that speech enduring by putting it into print. He whittles at the words and phrases of today and makes of them forms to set the mind of tomorrow's generation. That's history, and a writer is the architect of history."

Throughout his long career as one of America's best-known novelists, Dos Passos has remained true to his belief that a writer is an architect of history. Convinced that tomorrow's problems can best be solved by searching the past, he has dedicated his books to accurately portraying the sights and sounds of the world around him for future generations to see and understand. As a portrait of 20th-century America, Dos Passos' novels are unsurpassed.

Dos Passos believes that to realistically record the events of a generation, a writer must be an active participant in history. He fits well into his portrait of an author. His life reads like a novel, and from it he has drawn the basic ingredients for many of his stories.

Born in Chicago in 1896, the son of a Portuguese immigrant lawyer, Dos Passos was carted around a great deal as a child—to Mexico, Belgium, England, Washington, D.C., and to a farm in tidewater Virginia. After graduating from Harvard University, he went to Spain with the idea of studying architecture, but World War I broke out and he joined an ambulance service, later serving in the U.S. Medical Corps as a private.

These war experiences—especially the time spent as a vagabond ambulance driver, first in France, then in Italy —led to his first book, *One Man's Initiation*, published in 1920. Although filled with rage and disgust at the cruelty and inhumanity of war, the book attracted little attention from either critics or the public. His next work, however, *Three Soldiers*—a novel also debunking the so-called glory of World War I—won considerable literary acclaim and launched his writing career.

Seeker of Truth

Dos Passos emerged from the war as an independent seeker of truth, with the mission "to put the acid test to existing institutions, to strip them of their veils." He worked for a year as a newspaper correspondent and free-lance writer in Spain and Mexico but soon returned to America and lived in an apartment in New York's Greenwich Village.

In the next few years he carried over his disappointment with human nature born of his war experience into a series of biting novels about America. The first of these, *Manhattan Transfer*, brought Dos Passos great fame and still ranks as one of the best books ever written about New York—catching the elusive flavor of the city as it grew and changed from 1890 to 1925 and communicating a keen sense of its seething tempo.

In addition to being a realistic portrait of the large metropolis, *Manhattan Transfer* also expresses the author's sympathy with the plight of the individual pitted against demands from society which he is often unable to meet—a sympathy which led Dos Passos toward Marxism. Soon realizing, however, that monolithic systems and one-party states increase rather than solve mankind's ills, he abandoned all association with Marxist philosophy. Later he visited Soviet Russia, sharply criticizing its dictatorial communist practices and restrictions on individual freedom.

Studies America's Past

Although retaining an active interest in the cause of the individual throughout his long career, Dos Passos has been primarily concerned with writing a chronicle of his generation. To get proper perspective for his books, he began in the mid-1930's a serious study of America's past. As he read more and more about early statesmen and pioneers, his respect for democratic traditions—questioned during the war because of the suffering he saw—deepened, and he found much that could be applied to his own times.

In 1941, in *The Ground We Stand On*, Dos Passos wrote

about the lives and ideas of famous Americans in history. It was a call to his fellow countrymen to evaluate their own heritage—"the habits and traditions and skills of self-government"—and to recognize the totalitarian states abroad for what they were.

To keep himself up to date on America and therefore keep his novels and stories as realistic as possible, Dos Passos toured the country from 1942–43, setting down his impressions in *State of the Nation*. He found, and wrote, that America was "the country where the average guy got the better break," where people were free to "change their occupations, their way of living, their settlements as easily as they can eat their breakfasts."

"U. S. A."

Shortly after his trip across the nation, Dos Passos began a trilogy of novels entitled *U.S.A.* This trilogy, completed in 1949, remains his most outstanding work and has been acclaimed an eloquent portrait of American society during a significant period of national history.

A massive literary endeavor, *U.S.A.* depicts almost every aspect of life in the United States and follows some thirty characters through the first thirty years of this century. Because Dos Passos exerted as much effort to describe and make real the social scene as a traditional novelist would expend upon the development of a human hero, the actual protagonist in the trilogy is society itself. The many characters are subordinate to society—the essential point being the effect that the social and economic milieu has upon the individual.

To make this point clear, Dos Passos realized, the reader

must be given as vivid a picture of the era as possible. So he employed a variety of unconventional technical devices: the "newsreel," made up of snatches of popular songs, quotations from speeches, and reproductions of contemporary newspaper headlines; the "camera eye," snapshot flashes in free verse of his own experiences; and thumbnail biographical sketches of real persons whose activities coincided with those of his fictional creations.

"Midcentury"

After writing *U.S.A.*, Dos Passos' next major work was *Midcentury*, published in 1961 and subtitled by its publishers *A Contemporary Chronicle*— even though a work of fiction.

The book, comprising four integrated novels, portrays the present era just as *U.S.A.* described the early part of this century. Using his famous interplay of narrative fiction, borrowed headlines, midget biographies, and free verse, Dos Passos again captured a panoramic image of the United States.

Dos Passos' combination of history, biography, and fiction enables his readers to get a personalized look at their time and their contemporaries. And this is just what the author —tall, bald, and remote-looking behind thick glasses— wants them to get. For he has always believed that the problems of mankind will be solved by individual men in their own minds and hearts, and to help them he has presented a chronicle of history, a chance to learn from the past.

Today, his books—over thirty of them—add up to a portrait in words of modern America. Words are meant not merely to be read, however, but to be acted upon. Because, as Dos Passos once wrote, "The republic's foundations are not in the sound of words, they are in the shape of our lives."

—Bibliography—

PRINCIPAL WORKS: *Three Soldiers,* 1922; *Manhattan Transfer,* 1925; *U.S.A.* (trilogy consisting of three novels—*The 42nd Parallel,* 1930; *Nineteen Nineteen,* 1932; *The Big Money,* 1936), 1937; *The Ground We Stand On,* 1941; *The Great Days,* 1958; *The Shackles of Power,* 1966.

JOHN STEINBECK   (1902–1968)

Novelist of Dissent

JOHN STEINBECK, winner of the Nobel prize for literature
for 1962, was a big ruddy-faced man with a small graying
beard. Born in 1902 in the fruit orchard country of Salinas,
California, the son of a minor politician, Steinbeck took
little interest in formal education. Although he enrolled off
and on at Stanford University, he never graduated, dropping out from time to time to take odd jobs as farm hand,
newspaper reporter, and night watchman. Leaving California in his early twenties, he went to New York where he
began working on a newspaper, but soon he returned to his
native California orchard country to devote all of his time
to writing independently.

Struggling Young Author
Like most struggling young authors, Steinbeck couldn't

make a living with his pen, but fortunately he was able to get his food, mostly by fishing in the ocean. His first published novel, *Cup of Gold*, which told of the exploits of a sea pirate, was hardly noticed, but he kept trying. He recognized that if he were to win recognition as an author, he must write about the people he knew best—the farm community in the California valley where he lived. He told their stories, first in several short stories printed in book form as *The Pastures of Heaven* in 1932, and again a year later in a novel called *To a God Unknown*. These works were an improvement over his earlier writing, but they too attracted little attention, and it was not until 1935 when he wrote *Tortilla Flat*, a novel about California fruit pickers, that Steinbeck won critical recognition and some degree of popularity.

Spokesman of the Poor

Those early years of Steinbeck's writing career—the thirties—were a critical period in America. There were severe droughts and economic depression. Most Americans, especially farmers, had a difficult time. John Steinbeck, who had observed hardship in the California valley where he lived and wrote, became the spokesman of the unemployed, the poor, and the underprivileged. His novel *Grapes of Wrath* (1937) tells the story of an Oklahoma farm family who set out for California after losing their home through debt, and of their many hardships as they move from job to job—picking cotton and fruit, and eking out a bare living as best they could.

Although *Grapes of Wrath* expresses the despair of the period in which it was written, it closes on a note of hope and dignity. Ma Joad, a character of truly heroic mold, remains throughout the book a tower of strength, determined to keep her family together, confident that at last they will overcome their troubles. At the end, after her daughter gives birth during a storm to a stillborn child, Ma Joad says: "We ain't gonna die out. People is goin' on —changin' a little, maybe, but goin' right on."

Target of Critics

Grapes of Wrath won for Steinbeck the Pulitzer prize, was translated into thirty-three languages, and made him an international literary figure. Since that day his books have been highly publicized and widely read, but critics have disagreed over their merits. Some of his works have been termed "sentimental" and "pretentious." Steinbeck, at times, like many another author, struck back at his critics. In an interview with the press, after winning the Nobel prize, he said:

"It's a novelist's function to criticize, and to criticize means dissent. And it's an author's right to dissent from critics, especially when he's sure they haven't even read the work they're criticizing."

Steinbeck heard the news of his Nobel prize award one morning while watching TV at his home in Sag Harbor, New York. A few hours later, he visited his publisher's office in New York City to answer questions from reporters and critics. His replies were typical of Steinbeck, the man. Asked whether he deserved to win the Nobel prize, he answered, "Frankly, no." His favorite book, he said, was the one he was currently at work on. Asked by reporters what the book was about, he said, "If I talk it, I won't write it." Reporters asked about Steinbeck's work habits. He replied that he normally started writing about eight o'clock each day and continued until he had written between one thousand and three thousand words. He worked six days a week and sometimes seven. During the past thirty years, this daily word quota added up to twenty-seven books, mostly novels.

Steinbeck was reluctant to talk about himself, and once when asked for some autobiographic information, he said:

"Please feel free to make up your own facts about me as you need them. I can't remember how much of me really happened and how much I invented. ... Biography by its very nature must be half-fiction."

Praised by Academy

In awarding Steinbeck the Nobel prize, the Swedish Academy Committee singled out for special praise his novel published in 1961, *Winter of Our Discontent*, a lengthy work set in the New England states. In describing the novel, Doctor Anders Ursterling, permanent secretary of the academy, said:

"Steinbeck's realistic and imaginary writings are distinguished both by a sympathetic humor and a social perception. In John Steinbeck we find the American temperament expressed in his great feeling for nature, for the tilled soil, the wasteland, the mountains, and the ocean coasts—all an inexhaustible source of inspiration to Steinbeck in the midst of and beyond the world of human beings."

Steinbeck's "social perception" perhaps reached its greatest depth in *Grapes of Wrath*, but age and maturity tempered his later writing, revealing in him more of the American patriot than social critic—an author determined despite his age, the mid-sixties, not to let American history pass him by. Typical was his attitude toward the war in Vietnam. As the tempo of the fighting rose, Steinbeck yearned to be in the thick of it: to see, hear, and feel what his fellow Americans were doing in Vietnam. Arriving there in late 1966 as a war correspondent, he wrote in his paper, *Newsday*, a Long Island, N.Y. daily: "I would hate not to have a personal experience in the most important thing happening in our time."

His fatigues soaked with sweat, he slogged along with the troops knee-deep in mud; he explored booby-trapped tunnels, rode helicopters into the thick of Viet Cong territory, tried his hand at shooting weapons which ranged from an M-16 automatic rifle to an M-79 grenade launcher, and hobnobbed with America's Special Forces elite troops, the Green Berets, as they ranged the countryside in choppers, clearing out "the snakes."

Steinbeck quickly left no doubt whose side he was taking in the war. Comparing the Viet Cong to the notorious Mafia gangs of Italy, he wrote in one of his earlier columns: "Terror and torture are the Viet Cong's weapons. He bleeds the people he is saving of everything movable, kidnaps whole villages for forced labor, recruits the young men and holds the parents hostages. He murders any opposition noisily or secretly. He impales living bodies on sharpened stakes, slashes stomachs so that a man drags his intestines on the ground before he dies. . . ."

Steinbeck, the American patriot, was further revealed in his book *America and the Americans*, published in late 1966. The book, a seventy-page essay illustrated with pictures by fifty-five well-known contemporary photographers, describes the essences and paradoxes of America and Americans, and contains some of Steinbeck's best writing since the thirties. Here, in his own words, are some of the conclusions Steinbeck drew about his country and his fellow Americans:

"If I inspect my people and study them and criticize them, I must love them if I have any self-love, since I can never be separate from them and no more objective about them than I am about myself. I am not young, and yet I wonder about my tomorrow. How much more, then, must my wonder be about the tomorrow of my people, which is a young people. My questioning is compounded of some fear, more hope, and great confidence. . . .

"The world is open as it has never been before, and for the first time in human experience we have the tools to work with. Three-fifths of the world and perhaps four-fifths of the world's wealth lie under the sea, and we can get to it. The sky is open at last, and we have the means to rise into it. . . .

"We will make mistakes; we always have. But from our beginning, in hindsight at least, our social direction is clear. We have moved to become one people out of many. We have failed sometimes, taken wrong paths, paused for renewal, filled our bellies and licked our wounds; but we have never slipped back—never."

—Bibliography—

PRINCIPAL WORKS: *Cup of Gold*, 1929; *Tortilla Flat*, 1935; *Of Mice and Men*, 1937; *Grapes of Wrath*, 1939; *The Moon Is Down*, 1942; *Cannery Row*, 1945; *The Wayward Bus*, 1947; *East of Eden*, 1952; *Winter of Our Discontent*, 1961; *Travels with Charlie in Search of America*, 1962.

J. D. SALINGER   (1909–   )

Voice of Frustrated Youth

To THE YOUTH of America, J. D. Salinger perhaps speaks
with more magic than any other novelist in the United States
writing today. Salinger's ability to portray the inner turmoil, the frustrations, and the dreams of young people has
made him a popular topic of discussion at teen-age gather-
ings and on college campuses. His influence, however, is
far wider. He appeals also to many adults who find in his
writings an echo of the poignant, bittersweet experiences of
their own youth.

Prior to the publication in 1951 of *The Catcher in the Rye*,
Salinger had written a few short stories for leading American
magazines, but it was *The Catcher in the Rye*, which secured
for Salinger a place among America's top contemporary
authors.

Poet of Adolescence

The narrator and chief character of *The Catcher in the Rye* is sixteen-year-old Holden Caulfield, student at a military academy near New York City. Just before Christmas vacation, Holden, knowing that he is to be dropped by his school for making poor grades, decides to leave early and not to report home until he has to. He spends the next three days and nights in New York City, describing in his own words what he does and suffers there. In Holden's flight from "phonies" and his search for the good, the true, the real, a generation of young and not-so-young readers have recognized their own muddled search to find their way in our complex 20th-century society today. In the language of the novel—a combination of adolescent insight, prep-school slang, and poetry—they have found their own idiom. In fact, many people today speak of some of their experiences as being "like something out of a Salinger story."

Although *The Catcher in the Rye* was an immediate best seller, some found the frank language of the book offensive and some critics attacked it as being iconoclastic. Others felt that certain situations in the book lacked plausibility. The detractors were, however, a minority, and *Catcher* sold over 1.5 million copies in the United States. It also enjoyed a brisk sale in England, and in Finnish, Swedish, German, and Japanese translations.

To those who knew Salinger as a youngster, the fact that he is today one of America's leading men of letters must come as a surprise. Nothing in Salinger's early life indicated that he would one day gain prominence as an author. Born in 1919 in New York City, the son of a prosperous Jewish importer of hams, Salinger's IQ was an average 104 and his grades in school were not outstanding. Worried about his studies, his family enrolled him in a highly rated private school when he was thirteen, but he flunked out a year later. He did manage, however, to graduate from Valley Forge Military Academy in 1937 and later attended three universities, but he never earned a degree.

In 1942, Salinger was drafted into the Army and served with the 4th Infantry Division as a sergeant in counter-intelligence. He landed in Normandy just five hours after the initial assault and was with the 4th Division through the vicious fighting in Belgium during the Battle of the Bulge.

Hemingway Praised Talent

Salinger was an aloof, solitary soldier whose job it was to discover Gestapo agents by interviewing French civilians and German prisoners. In France, Staff Sergeant Salinger met famed author Ernest Hemingway, who read Salinger's work and remarked, "he has a helluva talent."

By 1946 Salinger was back in New York, rid not only of soldiering but of a brief, unsuccessful marriage to a European woman physician. He lived with his family and spent his evenings in Greenwich Village, New York's famous Bohemian quarter.

As Salinger became more engrossed in his work, he began a series of withdrawals. He lived for a while in Westport, Connecticut, home of many prominent artists and authors. Grumbling that "a writer's worst enemy is another author," he moved to a cottage on a ninety-acre tract in Corning, New Hampshire. In the winter he happily carried water from his stream and cut wood with a chain saw.

Married since 1955 to English-born Claire Douglas,

Salinger climaxed his withdrawal by building a high fence around his cottage and being at home only to close relatives and a handful of old friends. He spends his days writing in a cinder-block cubicle some one hundred yards from his house. In the evening he relaxes with his wife and their two children.

Saga of the Glass Family

Today Salinger is working on his first really large body of fiction, the saga of the Glass family, whose members have been the central characters in all of the stories he has written since 1955, and several before that time.

The elder Glasses are Irish-Jewish vaudevillians now retired to a life of comfortable reminiscence. Their seven children, too, have been professionals; they are all prodigies, and all appeared at one time or another on a radio quiz program.

The immense popularity of these stories is proved by the fact that when two of them which had previously been published in magazines were reprinted in book form as *Franny and Zooey*, many bookdealers sold out their initial stock in a matter of hours.

Turn to Religion

In his later Glass family stories and another short story, "Teddy," Salinger is no longer preoccupied with adolescence. The author's chief concern nowadays appears to be religion.

Since "Teddy"—an argument for the theory of reincarnation central to Mahayana Buddhism—his works seem to many not so much stories, or even poems, but religious tracts. Some friends believe that Salinger has become a Zen Buddhist, and that everything he does, thinks, or writes is influenced by Zen. Certainly much of his recent writing would bear them out.

Commenting on Salinger's work, the *Christian Science Monitor* stated the following: "Salinger's skill appears to be in setting up conflicts through which intellectual, aesthetic, and religious discussions assume biting overtones of humor and emotion. . . . It is the religious element that finally predominates."

Some critics believe that Salinger is using the members of the Glass family as spokesmen for various shades of religious experience—and hopes, when the saga of the Glass family is finished, to have written a definitive work on the religions of the world.

Slavish Devotion to His Work

Certainly Salinger has the seriousness of purpose to accomplish what he sets out to do. His isolation, although it may have neurotic overtones, is a form of almost slavish devotion to his work: he cannot stand to have it interrupted. The hours he spends writing are almost incredible to other authors. He rewrites, throws away, starts over again, but in the end his stories are as tight as violin strings. He is perhaps the greatest word-weaver in American literary history. His stories can be read, aside from any meaning they may or may not contain, as sheer poetry—which is perhaps what they are.

In explaining why he refuses to meet his public, the recluse Salinger once said, "The stuff is all in the stories; there is no use in talking about it."

—Bibliography—

PRINCIPAL WORKS: *The Catcher in the Rye*, 1951; *Nine Stories*, 1953; *Franny and Zooey*, 1961; *Raise High the Roof Beam, Carpenter*, 1965.

JOHN O'HARA   (1905–   )

Smooth Surface, with Depths

OF THE SERIOUS writers of contemporary American fiction, John O'Hara is perhaps the most prolific. Yet, despite the torrent of short stories, motion-picture scripts, plays, and novels which cascades from his typewriter, O'Hara maintains always the sure hand of a master craftsman.

"I want to get it all down on paper while I can," says O'Hara. "The United States in this century is what I know, and it is my business to write about it to the best of my ability, with the sometimes special knowledge that I have."

O'Hara's "special knowledge" is displayed in his books in a surprising array of people and things: saloon owners, political bosses, bums, mine owners, steel workers, stage and cinema stars, servants, doctors; brothels, college fraternities, hardware stores, and the exact amount of carbon monoxide necessary to kill a man in a garage. O'Hara has concentrated his multiple interests on depicting in detail the world of the very rich in the eastern United States in the first half of this century.

Manners, Rituals, and Rules

O'Hara's long concentration on the manners, the rituals, and the rules of behavior of the rich has led to the rather widespread assumption that his own background must be very poor, and a legend—touching but untrue—has come into being of the little waif who stood with nose pressed against the country-club window, and swore that he would one day go to an exclusive college and wear expensive clothes. This myth persists despite the fact that O'Hara himself has gone to some length to show it is fallacious. He has pointed out that his father was, in fact, a prosperous doctor in Pottsville, Pennsylvania, where John was born in 1905, and that his family was affluent enough to send him to some of the best preparatory schools in the U.S.

John O'Hara was a husky youth full of a lust for life and a hatred for the restraints of conformity. Unfortunately his nonconformist behavior kept him in hot water with the faculties of the various schools he attended, and he was expelled from several before finally winning a diploma.

Worked as Reporter

O'Hara's father died in 1925, after a series of bad investments had all but depleted the family fortune. As a result John abandoned his plans for attending college and instead supported himself by working as a reporter on his home-town newspaper. After three years as a small-town newsman, O'Hara invaded New York and found a job on a metropolitan daily. Over the next few years he worked on several newspapers and magazines in New York, being fired from most of them for taking unauthorized vacations.

From his first days in New York, O'Hara became a habitué of the better saloons, and he mixed effortlessly in the strange school of college boys, playboys, debutantes, show-business people, writers, and underworld executives that were their regular patrons in the thirties.

O'Hara's first short story appeared in *The New Yorker* magazine in 1928, and he immediately became a regular contributor. After five years as a successful short-story writer, he decided to try his hand at writing a novel. The novel, *Appointment in Samarra*, was a best seller and catapulted O'Hara into the front ranks of American authors.

Uncanny Eye for Detail

A brief, tightly constructed, fast-paced novel, *Appointment in Samarra* has the virtues that have characterized O'Hara's work ever since: the direct, colloquial prose, unadorned by metaphor or simile, faultless touch with dialogue, and an uncanny eye for detail.

The setting for *Appointment* and many of his other works is "Gibbsville, Pennsylvania," modeled on O'Hara's home town of Pottsville. O'Hara has always seen Pottsville, or "Gibbsville," not as a special case but as a microcosm of the eastern United States; its citizens create and react to the same kinds of social patterns as their counterparts in Harrisburg, New York or Philadelphia. The same forces of wealth, class, and tradition operate in each, overlaid on the primal forces within the individual, and O'Hara has made it his business to examine all of it.

"I Want to Record with . . . Honesty and Variety"

Portraying this complex and compellingly interesting world of the rich in the first half of this century is the task that O'Hara has set for himself. He says, "The '20s, '30s, and the '40s are already history, but I cannot be content to leave their story in the hands of the historians and the editors of picture books. I want to record the way people talked and thought and felt, and to do it with complete honesty and variety."

O'Hara's world is a world that not very many people know, elegant and deceptively placid on the surface, and stocked almost casually with large houses and luxurious country clubs, superior cars, horses, and servants, and men's clubs that blackball very few men because so few are ever put up for membership. The inhabitants are less easily described, but there are some things about them which may be said to be generally true: money or power is not an appurtenance, like a good hat, but a part of them, like blood, and they are neither miserly nor spendthrift about it. Very few of the inhabitants are religiously pious, and even fewer are intellectuals, but all of them have a sense of security about their place in the world that is unshakable.

The Real Texture of Things

To this gift for sociological insight, O'Hara adds a passionate concern for the real texture of things. In preparing for a novel, he will often pore through hundreds of old newspapers and magazines, looking not only for important historical data but for the everyday reality of real-estate prices, dress-hem lengths, auto styles, play openings, and lapel widths.

As one critic said, "When he names a make of car or a brand of luggage or a variety of wearing apparel, we can be sure that he has the right article in the right place at the right time."

But, although he has always sought to be lifelike, O'Hara has never copied life. In a period in which symbolism and fantasy have become highly regarded and realism in fiction less fashionable, he has come as close to pure realism as a serious writer can.

Professional Pride

O'Hara matches his unfashionable penchant for realism with an enormous productivity unusual at any time, but especially striking in this century when many celebrated writers go for decades without publishing anything. His most recent novel, *Elizabeth Appleton*, for instance, marks O'Hara's twenty-second book and tenth novel since he first won fame in 1934 with *Appointment in Samarra*.

Now past sixty, O'Hara for some years has been listening to hints that he slow down, but he has reasons for ignoring them. One is that he genuinely likes to write, and couples this liking with a fierce sense of professional pride. Another is that his books sell about as well as those of any serious writer now living. His books, in all editions, have sold something like fifteen million copies in the U.S. and have been translated into nearly every civilized tongue.

For whatever reason, O'Hara's capacity for work shows no signs of failing. Five or six days a week at about one P.M., he enters his study and settles himself in a leather swivel chair behind his desk. From then until late into the night or sometimes until dawn, he types cleanly and rapidly on the typewriter on his desk. He writes one draft—of a short story or a novel, it makes no difference—without carbon, virtually without pencil changes, and sends it off to be published.

"For the last ten years," he has said, "my whole life has been in this house—in this room, really." He adds, "I don't want to sound pompous, but I do have pride as a writer, and I feel I have a duty to get down as much of what I know as I can."

—Bibliography—

PRINCIPAL WORKS: *Appointment in Samarra*, 1934; *Butterfield 8*, 1935; *Hope of Heaven*, 1938; *Pal Joey*, 1940; *A Rage to Live*, 1949; *Ten North Frederick*, 1955; *From the Terrace*, 1958; *Elizabeth Appleton*, 1963; *The Lockwood Concern*, 1965.

SAUL BELLOW (1915–   )

Alienation Is for the Birds

IN AN ERA in which alienation has been called the great
20th-century malaise and bookshops are crowded with
volumes diagnosing the ills of our complex, machine-driven
age, a new voice has risen to champion the dignity and
worth of modern man. The voice is that of Saul Bellow,
whose novel *Herzog* headed the best-seller list in the United
States for several months in 1964–65.

Deploring the tendency of modern writers to underrate
mankind, Bellow says: "I do not believe that the human
capacity to feel and to do can really have dwindled or the
quality of humanity has degenerated. I rather feel that
people appear small because society has become so immense.
Hugest of all are the fears that surround us. They keep us from
realizing our proper size and the importance of our deeds."

Bellow's *Herzog* is a clear departure from what the author

calls "victim literature"—that school of the modern novel which purports to show the impotence of modern man. Herzog is a fighter who stubbornly refuses to surrender to the pitfalls and complications of modern society.

As the novel opens, Herzog—once a distinguished professor of English and author of a brilliant academic work—is a man at the end of his wits. He has gone from one personal disaster to another: twice divorced, betrayed by his friends, banished from his children, unemployed, and broke.

He wanders about distracted. He visits in his imagination the scenes of his childhood, his broken marriages, his broken career. He disappears from New York and flies to Chicago, where, gun in hand, he spies through a window at his ex-wife's lover bathing one of Herzog's small daughters. Herzog, however, lacks the swift decision of an assassin. At last he comes back to his only remaining property, a decaying farmhouse in a depopulated area in Massachusetts.

Herzog, in short, is a failure, one of the losses of our time, a battered man at the edge of sanity. Throughout his mental and physical wandering, he composes letters—to friends and enemies, professional rivals and colleagues, to the President of the United States, to philosophers Spinoza and Nietzsche, and to God. The letters are cranky, brilliant, poignant, and, of course, never mailed. However, in the course of composing them, Herzog comes at last to accept himself and his life. He finds redemption.

Born in Canada

The author who created Herzog, Saul Bellow, was born on July 10, 1915, in Quebec, Canada, two years after his immigrant Jewish parents arrived from Russia. A few years later the family moved to Chicago, where Bellow attended the University of Chicago for two years (1933–35), and later Northwestern University where he received a degree in anthropology in 1937. That year he did postgraduate work at the University of Wisconsin but quit school to marry Anita Goshkin. He resolved to be a writer, meanwhile earning a living as an editorial worker for the *Encyclopædia Britannica*. He published two novels, *Dangling Man* (1944) and *The Victim* (1947), both commercial failures, and it was not until a third novel, *The Adventures of Augie March*, was issued in 1953 that Bellow's work won favor with the public.

The Adventures of Augie March is a sprawling, picaresque novel about a light-fingered, opportunistic Chicagoan. Up from the depths of poverty to the heights of success, back down, back up, and all in most peculiar fashion—that is Augie March. The story at times comes close to being a mere catalogue of actions: jobs, journeys, jolts, women, crime, labor unions and society, thievery, and high honor.

The *New York Times* had this to say about *Augie:* "In writing a long, picaresque novel, Mr. Bellow goes back to the earliest and most generic form of the novel. It is a form which has always been convenient to observant humorists who relish human variety, who are fertile in creating characters and who are not afraid to seem more interested in life than in art."

Calm and Modest

Bellow today is remarkably calm, modest, and self-assured. Of medium height and build, he has doleful, heavy-lidded eyes, a straight nose, graying hair, and a kind of battered good looks. His is an expressive face, and it expresses much of the life that he has seen and understood. Like his protagonist, Herzog, he has the brooding air of a man who has been through a lot.

Asked once why he decided to become a writer, Bellow said he had chosen the vocation through innocence. "I will say this for my choice," he added, "there are many professions that one may follow without enthusiasm, but, though there may be as many unenthusiastic novelists, proportionately, as there are unenthusiastic dentists and engineers, they must consider themselves infidels and they feel their unbelief and treason keenly. Vividness is what they must desire most and so they must value human existence or be unfaithful to their calling."

Prefers Quiet Life

The reception accorded to *Herzog* was, of course, very pleasing to Bellow. "But," he says, "one has to choose between playing the social role and being a writer." He carefully avoids literary circles, preferring to live quietly in Chicago with his family.

Despite his success as a novelist, Bellow continues to teach at the University of Chicago in the Committee for Social Thought, a special graduate program that includes some of America's most distinguished thinkers. Bellow enjoys teaching but reserves his afternoons for writing. In addition to his novels, he has contributed much literary criticism and numerous commentaries to leading magazines.

One of the more erudite contemporary writers, Bellow is a voracious reader. But it is not his vast knowledge on a large variety of subjects or his great fame as an author that his friends talk about. It is his warmth and humor and his gift as a raconteur that they mention most often. His circle includes old boyhood friends who hardly know that he is an author. His loyalty extends also to his Jewish identity. Bellow takes pleasure in his Jewish background and has an excellent command of Yiddish.

Those who know Bellow best claim that his philosophy of life is summed up in the words of Herzog, who after long suffering comes to the conclusion that, "I am pretty well satisfied to be, to be just as it is willed, and for as long as I remain in occupancy."

—Bibliography—

PRINCIPAL WORKS: *Dangling Man*, 1944; *The Victim*, 1947; *The Adventures of Augie March*, 1953; *Herzog*, 1964.